This book belongs to
Lindsey Graham Green

395

Flames of the Spirit

Flames of the Spirit

Resources for Worship

Edited by Ruth C. Duck

The Pilgrim Press
Cleveland, Ohio

97 96 95 94   10 9 8 7 6

Library of Congress Cataloging-in-Publication Data
Main entry under title:

Flames of the spirit.

Resources based on the lectionary and the liturgical year.
1. Church year.   2. Worship programs.
I. Duck, Ruth C., 1947-
BV30.F55   1985   264   85-6596
ISBN 0-8298-0537-0 (pbk.)

Contents

Preface

God comes to us as a burning fire that does not consume,
a revelation bringing warmth and vitality.*

The call to worship is a call to kindle, without ceasing, the awareness of God's fiery presence among us.

The flames of God's Spirit bring vitality to our lives together in the church. Without the Spirit, our lives are dry and dead like leaves fallen from a tree. The Spirit takes our dryness and brittleness and sets burnt-out Christians on fire with love that is always new.

I believe it was D. T. Niles who said, "The church exists by mission as a fire by burning." John Wesley, who spoke of his heart being strangely warmed by God's Spirit, was compelled by the Spirit to serve the poor and suffering in his land. The flames of the Spirit kindle in us love not only for God, but for all those whom God loves.

God spoke to Moses out of a burning bush that was not consumed by fire, calling him to lead his people to freedom. A fiery pillar served as light to lead the people through the wilderness. The flames of the Spirit still lead us in the journey of liberation, the journey toward a new world where people of all races, tongues, and nations live in a just peace.

"Give me oil in my lamp, keep me burning, burning, burning," says an old spiritual. Continually, Christians must return to the warm center of worship to be renewed in their courage to accept the cost and joy of discipleship in the world. In worship we reflect on what is past and kindle visions of what is to come, all in the light of God's word, that we may live as God's people in the world. According to Luke, John the Baptist said that the one who would come after him would baptize with the Holy Spirit and with fire; and when the flames of the Spirit did come on the disciples they were given power to witness and serve in Jesus' name.

May these worship resources enable congregations, as they gather, to come alive to the Spirit of love, freedom, and justice, and enable them to depart with a burning desire to be God's people in the world.

Much of the material included in this book came in response to a notice in *Keeping You Posted*, a newspaper of the United Church of Christ. Contributors are UCC, United Methodist, Lutheran, and Presbyterian; they are students, pastors, and members of worship committees. They live in varied geographical areas of the United States. Among them are a seminary professor, an artist, a youth group, two church executives, three doctoral students, a checkout clerk, several

---

*Lavon Bayler, Lenten Call to Worship, page 30 of this book.

college professors and chaplains, and many, many local church pastors. All told, there are fifty-four authors from almost that many worship settings.

I am grateful that my first book of worship resources, *Bread for the Journey*, has been used so widely. People who have used that book will find *Flames of the Spirit* to be similar in style but different in organization. I chose the material on the basis of its quality rather than seeking to provide calls to worship or unison prayers for every Sunday of the church year. Therefore, there may be more or fewer prayers for a season than there are Sundays. When material did not seem limited in its use to one season, I placed it in the general section, hoping that this new approach would be helpful to worship leaders. These changes made it possible to offer more material than would have been the case otherwise.

Special thanks to Barbara Peterson, who has been my assistant in this project (doing research, correspondence, and typing), and to Sally Day, who typed the final manuscript. As always, thanks to Marion Meyer of The Pilgrim Press, for her wise and gentle guidance.

"Do not put out the Spirit's fire," Paul told the church at Thessalonica (1 Thess. 5:19, NIV). May the flames of the Spirit always enlighten the life, worship, and witness of the church of Jesus Christ.

Ruth Duck

Resources Based on the Lectionary and the Liturgical Year

Advent

A. Litanies of the Advent Candles

First Sunday

LEADER: Christians around the world begin this day to await the advent of Christ. We join with a joyous and hopeful throng in lighting the Advent candles, symbols of our faith and signs of God's love.

PEOPLE: We gather as a people of Hope.

LEADER: Christian people around the world stand today in breathless anticipation of a miracle that has been repeated for hundreds of years, yet that astounds us anew each year.

PEOPLE: Our hope springs anew, from an ancient vision.

LEADER: As we light the first Advent candle, let it stand for hope based not on wishful thinking, but on deep conviction. We believe, we have seen, we have received the Promise and the Great Gift, and therefore, in the midst of darkness and imperfection, we hope.

PEOPLE: We gather expectantly, joyfully, and with deep commitment, for we have heard that a special Child is to come, that God is to be among us, and that soon we will see a new creation on earth. We are a people of hope.

Lighting of the Candle of Hope (RDS)

Second Sunday

LEADER: The season of Advent continues. Four thousand years of waiting for the Messiah, commemorated by the lighting of four candles.

PEOPLE: We join with a hopeful throng in the lighting of the Advent candles, symbols of our faith and signs of God's love.

LEADER: We are a people of hope. Last Sunday the frail light of a single candle dared to pierce through the darkness of desolation and sin.

PEOPLE: Hope lives in us and will abide with us.

LEADER: Today we will light the candle of peace.

PEOPLE: This light, too, must brave great darkness.

LEADER: In an age when people so seldom find peace within themselves, and when all the earth stands under threat of total annihilation, we light a fire called peace.

PEOPLE: Peace that is not merely the absence of war and conflict, but peace that is the fullness of blessing for all—that is the peace for which we dare to hope.

LEADER: The Christ comes to bring peace to those who have been separated from God and one another.

PEOPLE: In the name of that Child born so long ago, we light the candle of peace.

LEADER: In following Christ's teachings, we nurture our hope for peace even today.

Lighting of the candles of Hope and Peace (MSG)

Third Sunday *(Alludes to John 3:16, RSV)*

LEADER: God is making the final preparations for an amazing thing! Now is the Advent of the long-awaited Messiah, our bringer of hope, our Prince of Peace, our leader of love.

PEOPLE: We wait, we prepare, we make straight the way.

LEADER: We celebrate the coming of Christ with the lighting of the Advent candles.

PEOPLE: We are a people of hope, a people of peace, a people of love.

LEADER: At first there was the frail light of a single candle of hope, daring to pierce through the darkness of despair and sin,

PEOPLE: Then there was the candle of peace, the gentle and persistent fire, the one that calls out the violent forces and lets in God's deep and tranquil Spirit.

LEADER: Today we light the candle of love. No other word so adequately captures the spirit and goal of our faith. No other word so completely describes what we know of our God.

PEOPLE: For God so loved the world . . .

LEADER: For God so loved the world that a child was given. A savior was made in the form of Love Incarnate. And Love was allowed to live on . . .

PEOPLE: We gather, then, in Christian Love;

LEADER: We give thanks for a love that passes understanding, and we await the dawning of God's pervasive and enduring love once more this Christmas season. Amen.

Lighting of the candles of Hope, Peace, and Love (RDS)

Fourth Sunday *(Paraphrases the hymn "Joy to the World")*

LEADER: Joy to the world!

PEOPLE: This, then, is the culmination of our years of waiting.

LEADER: We have lit the candles of hope, of peace, of love. In the glow of their light we feel the warmth of deep and quiet joy.

PEOPLE: Joy to the earth, the Savior reigns.

LEADER: Let us our songs employ.

PEOPLE: Let us sing to the glory of God;

LEADER: Let us sing in the name of Christ who offers us hope in the prison of despair,

PEOPLE: Peace in the chaos of life,
LEADER: God's love—graciously, silently, vulnerably offered.
PEOPLE: And heaven, and heaven and nature sing.
Lighting of the Advent candles of Hope, Peace, Love, and Joy   (MSG)

B. Calls to Worship

1. (*First Sunday in Advent, Year C; alludes to Ephesians 5:8 and 1 Thessalonians 5:5,* RSV)
   LEADER: Watch! Wait! The day of God is at hand!
   PEOPLE: Like the bud on a tree, God's possibilities are about to blossom!
   LEADER: Stay awake! The reign of God is very near.
   PEOPLE: We are here, watching and waiting with hope. May God bring justice to all people this very day. We rejoice in God as children of the Light!   (SEG)

2. LEADER: Come, let us be about our preparations for a new advent of love among us.
   PEOPLE: The wastelands of life around us cannot shut out the promise of life-giving water.
   LEADER: Hatred and warfare, injustice and suffering, are not the last word, for they are not of God.
   PEOPLE: We hear again the promise of peace, coming in the one who lived Shalom among all people.
   LEADER: We see again the light God promises in the midst of our darkness.
   PEOPLE: We are feeling again the joy that comes through partnership in the gospel.
   LEADER: May our worship recall us to what is centered in life; to the One who gives us breath and purpose in life.
   PEOPLE: We come to embrace the new advent, to be renewed in faith, hope, and love.   (LB)

3. (*Quotes Isaiah 9:2,* RSV)
   LEADER: The people who walked in darkness have seen a great light.
   PEOPLE: The light shines even in the places where shadows touch our lives.
   LEADER: Rejoice, then, you people, for Christ's presence lives among us,
   PEOPLE: And brings light to our world.   (SEG)

C. Invocations

1. O God, this Advent season is a time when your light radiates through the world. Inasmuch as we can, let us be bright for you.

   Shine your light through us as though we were pieces in a stained-glass window. Flow through us into others as the warm glow of colors seeps into a church.

Fill us with your light as though we were lighthouses on the shore. Use us to guide others and to keep them from danger.

Set us aflame with your light as though we were candles, even candles in a storm. Enable us to burn steadily with your fiery Spirit and to push aside all forms of darkness.

Turn us on with your light as though we were Christmas bulbs all connected to one another. Help us as a community of faith to celebrate the sparkling good news of your Son's coming birth.

Be present with us, God, throughout the Advent season as we live and worship in our wait for the One who is the world's light. Amen.   (GER)

2. Come, Christ Jesus, be our guest,
   and may our lives by you be blest.

   Come, God-with-us,
   and free us from the false claims
   of the empires of this world.
   We are lonely for you and your peace.

   Come, Emmanuel, and dwell with us,
   Make us your people indeed,
   the people through whom you bring
   love and justice to the world.

   Come, Jesus, and reign;
   Claim your rightful place in our hearts
   and in the midst of our community.
   Plant the seeds of hope among us.
   Establish God's reign on earth.

   For we pray as you taught us
   that God's reign might come in fullness on earth.

Prayer of Our Savior   (RCD)

D. Unison Prayers

1. (*First Sunday in Advent, Year C; alludes to Revelation 22:16; 1 Thessalonians 5:5; and Ephesians 5:8;* RSV)   O God, you never sleep but always watch with infinite care over your children. Keep us from growing weary of waiting for your love, lest we miss the glory of your appearing. O Christ, bright morning star, awaken us to live today as children of the light. Even so, come quickly, to our lives and our world. Amen.   (RCD)

2. Gentle God, you know that for us, this is a season of hopes and fears. We are caught up in our excitement and plans. We worry whether everything will get done, and whether our relationships will blossom, bend, or break in the stress of the season. Slow us down, God, and help us to place our hope in you. Be our

calm center, that we may be channels of peace to the people around us; through the grace of Jesus Christ. Amen.   (RCD)

3. Eternal Source of birth and new life, help us to prepare ourselves for the coming of Christ. Smooth out our roughness when it hurts ourselves or others. Lift up the hidden parts of ourselves—the talents, the visions, the tenderness—so that your love may be seen and your glory revealed among us. As this season unfolds, help us, like Mary, your servant, to rejoice in your surprising love. Amen.   (RCD)

4. God of Advent, we live in the promise that you will fulfill your will for earth. Yet nations are in chaos and our lives in turmoil. Gather us together to begin our watch for the coming of your Promised One. Lead us through the chaos by a watchful heeding spirit. In the name of the One who is to come, we pray. Amen.   (JCW)

5. (*Third Sunday in Advent, Year A; alludes to Matthew 11:2–15 and James 5:7–10*, RSV)   God of all hopefulness, help us to keep alive your vision of peace and wholeness. Where hope is a small seed, teach us to have faith in its growing. Where people are finding healing and new life, teach us to recognize you at work. When you come to us in unexpected ways, may we know you, through the grace of Jesus Christ. Amen.   (RCD)

E. Prayers of Confession

1. Call to Confession

The cares of this life weigh us down, and we seek escape more than insight, avoidance rather than confrontation with God's truth. God comes to us even when we are hiding from the best we know. God waits to hear our story and to restore us to life as it is meant to be. Let us come to God in prayer.

Prayer of Confession

We confess, Surprising God, that our sense of anticipation has been dulled. We have ceased to expect any wonders from your hand. We do not see the marvels around us in the people and happenings we view as commonplace. We are not alert to your presence or your action on our behalf. Wake us up, God, lest sleep be our death. Pardon and redeem us, that we may escape the judgment we are bringing on ourselves. Send your light that it may shine through us into a needy world. In Jesus' name, Amen.   (LB)

2. God of light, who shines in deepest darkness, we hear you calling us out of hopelessness into hope. But we are frightened by your call. We are afraid of taking chances; we are afraid of following your light, because it leads us into the places where you need us. We don't want to see how your people hurt. We don't want to see your light shining in the eyes of our neighbor. Yet we know that in those places your grace shines; help us to seek your light. Guide us in your way,

that we might be your children of day. Through the Light of the World, we pray. Amen. (SEG)

LEADER: God is light! In God there is no darkness! Arise! Shine! Our Light awaits!
PEOPLE: We are forgiven. Our future awaits us with hope. We will walk in the light of God's grace! Alleluia! Amen! (SEG)

3. God of grace, you send signs of love in people who care. But often we shut those people out. We turn away your love when we need it the most. We deny your hope within us, and we keep ourselves isolated and afraid. Visit us with your salvation, for we await you in need. Amen. (SEG)

F. Litanies

1. (*Alludes to the hymn "O Come, Emmanuel" and to Isaiah 11:1; Revelation 22:16; and John 14:6;* RSV)
LEADER: O come, Emmanuel, come to us, for we are lonely for God.
PEOPLE: Come, bring the peace of God-with-us.
LEADER: O come, Wisdom from on high,
PEOPLE: Lead us in the ways of knowledge, and show us the paths of peace.
LEADER: Glorious Shoot from the Jesse tree,
PEOPLE: Come, and bring life, fresh and green and lovely, to our spirits.
LEADER: O Rose which blooms in the snow of winter,
PEOPLE: Come, and grant to us the blessed gift of hope.
LEADER: O Bright Morning Star of the darkened world,
PEOPLE: Come and be for us the Light, the Truth, and the Way.
ALL: Jesus our Christ, we welcome you. Come and be known among us, for we want to be your people. Amen. (RCD)

2. (*Alludes to John 1:5 and Ephesians 3:21,* RSV)
LEADER: Christ has come.
Christ was dead.
Christ has risen.
Christ will come again.
PEOPLE: This is the faith of the Church of Jesus Christ.
LEADER: When we look at the world around us, we see the darkness of war, captivity, greed, and broken relationships.
PEOPLE: We long for Christ to come again and bring light to the world.
LEADER: Yet the word of the gospel is that Jesus Christ lives among us, bringing truth and light as a present reality.
PEOPLE: We worship as those who have a glimpse of that realm and long for its fullness; and as those who labor to make its light more visible on earth.
ALL: Let us praise God that the light of Christ shines on in the darkness, which has never overcome it. To God be glory in Jesus Christ and in the church forever and ever. Amen. (RCD)

G. Benedictions

1. LEADER: Go forth from this place an awakened people, aware of the world's darkness, yet reaching for the light.

   PEOPLE: We see God at work in our world, and that makes all the difference.

   LEADER: Go forth from this place an expectant people, conscious of judgment in our midst, yet welcoming God's new order and justice.

   PEOPLE: We welcome God's new day, believing that Christ will set us free.

   LEADER: Go forth from this place a serving people, sensing anew the pain so many bear, yet confident God will bring healing, even through you.

   PEOPLE: We open ourselves as channels of God's grace, for we have heard good news and we have been empowered to share it.

   LEADER: Amen.

   PEOPLE: Amen.   (LB)

2. Stir up your power, O God, and with your great might come among us.
Bring the Christ to us and deliver us. Amen.   (HAS)

3. (*Quotes Isaiah 55:12, RSV; alludes to Isaiah 35:4, RSV, and Revelation 22:20,*
KJV)   You shall go out in joy, and be led forth in peace.
The mountains and the hills before you shall break forth into singing, and all the trees of the fields shall clap their hands.
For your God comes, powerful to save.
Even so, come quickly to our world and to our lives.
Amen.   (RCD)

4. Follow the light of hope's guiding star. Seek the child.
Listen to the words of a heavenly host. Find the child.
Offer as gifts the best that you have. Serve the child.
Peace be among us. God be with us. Amen.   (GER)

H. Pastoral Prayer/Prayer for One Voice

(*Begin with a period of silent prayer—allowing us to become centered and to focus on that which concerns us most, our needs to say thanks and to seek help.*)
Most gracious God—receive these our prayers.

We admit that it is difficult to be silent and to focus—especially during this season—for we want too much and want to do so much. You already know how our expectations exceed reality and how our hopes and desires surpass possibility. Yet, even as we confess this, we celebrate this season filled with hope and expectation of that beyond our most creative imagination. God, we thank you for this time and for the gift of Advent which stirs and excites us.

We pray for the gift of light which we celebrate at Christmas. We do need light, O God; we are people who walk in darkness—living by trial and error, bouncing from one obstacle to another, stumbling, groping, hoping, failing, falling—sometimes we even walk in circles to avoid the unfamiliar which we fear as darkness.

We have tried to generate our own light—using our minds and our best resources to make sense out of life. We have written laws to protect it—and us, we've called councils and composed creeds to uphold it, and we've lived by following our own ways. But—hard as it is to admit—our light is not enough. We still have wars and people are hungry and hurt, afraid and running, alone and unhappy with the darkness closing in.

God, forgive us. Turn us on to the Light of Life, the Light of the World, whose coming we celebrate as the gift of Christmas . . . let us receive it.

We pray also for the gift of love—love is also what we need, O God. For we are people who are starving for love. We live as if love can be made or controlled, or as if we don't need it at all. Then we wonder why we feel empty, tired, and alone . . .

God, forgive us. Help us to be open to your love—the love which we celebrate at Christmas as that which empowers and frees, forgives and renews, heals and comes to us regardless . . . God, let us receive it.

Because we need to and because we trust your gifts, we also lift up these our prayers, not only for ourselves but also for others in this one world:

—For those who are anxious and afraid . . .

—For those who are ill . . .

—For those who are facing difficult decisions . . .

—For those who are feeling left out and are alone . . .

—For those who are mourning losses, especially those who are feeling deeply because of seasons past . . .

—And those who are feeling especially grateful and are filled with joy because of new news.

Gentle God, you know us and all about us. Help us to know you and all about you in new ways that will assure us and free us to live gratefully and hopefully—today, tomorrow, and every day and morrow.

In the name of Jesus, we pray. Amen.

(ARE)

Christmas and Christmastide

A. Calls to Worship

1. *(Paraphrases Luke 1:47, 49–53, RSV; Luke 2:14, KJV; and Matthew 5:6, RSV)*

   LEADER: Let our spirits rejoice in God our Savior, who has done great things for us, and for all people.

   PEOPLE: God scatters the proud in the imagination of their hearts, and raises up those who humble themselves.

   LEADER: God fills the hungry with good things and satisfies those who thirst for goodness.

   ALL: Glory be to God in the highest, and on earth, peace and goodwill to all. Amen.
   (RCD)

2. LEADER: God calls us now in this Christmas season to become new,
   PEOPLE: To make room for our own nativity, even where there is no room at the inn.
   LEADER: Where we are busy—
   PEOPLE: Peace.
   LEADER: Where we are lost—
   PEOPLE: Salvation.
   LEADER: Where we are sad—
   PEOPLE: Joy.
   LEADER: Where we are bitter—
   PEOPLE: Love.
   LEADER: Let this hour be a time to hope for all these gifts of God. Amen.

   (RDS)

3. (*Paraphrases Isaiah 9:2*, RSV)
   LEADER: Out of the busyness of our worlds,
   PEOPLE: Out of the crankiness and boredom of life-as-usual—
   LEADER: Out of the darkness, we have seen a great light.
   PEOPLE: Those who dwelt in a land of deep darkness: On them has light shined.
   LEADER: The birth of a baby calls us to something special.
   PEOPLE: Let our worship be our new beginning. Amen.   (RDS)

4. (*Paraphrases Philippians 2:6–7, 10–11*, RSV; *quotes Luke 2:14*, RSV)
   LEADER: Let us celebrate Christmas in the Spirit of Jesus Christ, who came to us from the heart of God's own being, taking the form of a servant, being born in human likeness.
   PEOPLE: Like Jesus, we would seek at this season more to give than to receive, and more to love than to be loved.
   LEADER: We celebrate God's entering into our lives in human form, to bring light to all the world.
   ALL: May every knee bow before the newborn Savior; with the angels, may every tongue sing: Glory to God in the highest. Amen.

   (RCD)

5. (*Christmas Eve; paraphrases Luke 2:10–11*, RSV)
   LEADER: Have you not heard? Something new has happened upon our earth!
   PEOPLE: Yes, we have heard! Rumors say there has been a child born, a Savior given!
   LEADER: People of God, these are not rumors. For unto us is born this day in Bethlehem Christ our Savior!
   PEOPLE: This is good news of great joy which has come to all people!
   UNISON: Let us go see this Savior of God and bring gifts of praise! Let us then go to Bethlehem.
   (May be followed by "O Little Town of Bethlehem")   (JCW)

19

6. (*Christmas Eve; quotes Isaiah 9:2*, RSV)
    LEADER: Tonight on Christmas Eve we kneel with families all over the earth in the presence of the Most High.
    PEOPLE: The people who walked in darkness have seen a great light; those who dwelt in a land of deep darkness, on them has light shined.
    LEADER: As we have been invaded by light, let us enlighten.
    PEOPLE: As we have been found, let us seek out the lost.
    LEADER: As we have been liberated, let us set the captives free.
    UNISON: For to us a child is born, One whom God sends to bring peace and light, freedom and reconciliation. Thanks be to God. Amen.

(HWW)

B. Unison Prayers

1. (*Christmas Eve*)   God who labors to bring forth abundant life among us, we thank you for the birth we celebrate tonight. A newborn bundle of human life can cause us to gaze for hours, amazed. Refresh our amazement that you sent Jesus to us from your very self, to be born as a human baby, and to live among us, showing us the way to new life. In response to your great labor of love, may we open ourselves to you, that you may create new life among us. In Jesus' name we pray. Amen.

(RCD)

2. (*Christmas; paraphrases 1 Corinthians 1:25*, RSV)   Loving God, you have come to us, not with great signs and wonders, but in a babe who became a humble carpenter. You took on human form, not with the trappings of power and might, but among folk who fasted, prayed, and gave thanks in the midst of their poverty. You made your witness, not with devices of intimidation and coercion, but through an instrument of suffering and scorn. For your foolishness is wiser than human thought, and your weakness is stronger than all human powers. Grant that we may hear and respond to your wisdom, O God. Amen.

(LB)

C. Offertory Prayer

Thank you, God of love, for the promise of this season. We are grateful for the generosity aroused in us by Christ's coming into the world. May these gifts represent a new spirit of joyous sharing among us, for the sake of all your children everywhere. Amen.

(LB)

D. Doxology for Christmas

Praise God whose dawn transfigures night,
Whose Daystar shines for us on high,
Whose Spirit brings into our sight
The hope which to our world draws nigh. Amen.

(DBB)

E. Litany

LEADER: The world is decked in the garb of celebration:
PEOPLE: Tinsel and lights, garlands of greenery, brightly colored packages and flashing Christmas greetings cover our world.
LEADER: The world is engaged in the spirit of celebration:
PEOPLE: Festive singing, fine food, merry parties, and grand traditions abound.
LEADER: Yet the best efforts fall short,
PEOPLE: For it is the birth of the Messiah we celebrate.
LEADER: It is the incarnation of God.
PEOPLE: How can we respond to the greatness of this event?
LEADER: How can we celebrate the Messiah's birth?
PEOPLE: We celebrate in worship.
LEADER: Christmas is a time of worship. It is the moment when the busiest of us pause in wonder.
PEOPLE: Let us worship together! (SRH)

F. Christmas Eve Communion

(Alludes to John 1:14; James 1:17; Exodus 32:13; and 2 Timothy 1:10; RSV)

The Invitation

Unison Prayer of Confession

Light of the World: you gave us the transforming birth of the child Jesus as a light for our path. Yet we confess that we shut our eyes to the light. We admit that we do not want to see the gift you have given us. We acknowledge our reluctance to see and share our gifts with our sisters and brothers. We are often dazzled by the glitter and tinsel the world has made of Christ's birth. We ask that your Spirit be lit within us, that we may share your gifts of peace and justice with all people. We seek to receive, and return the gift of Christ's birth and death, again and again. Amen.

Words of Assurance

Litany of Remembrance and Consecration

LEADER: God of light, in whom there is no shadow, your gifts to us are from the very beginning of time.
PEOPLE: They began with creation, when your Spirit gave form to the chaos of energy and matter, and when your word brought forth light on the face of the earth.
LEADER: They continued with our ancient ancestors, like Noah, whom you blessed with the colorful promise of the rainbow,
PEOPLE: And like Sarah and Abraham, whom you blessed with a child whose descendants, as many as the stars of the sky, were to be a light to the nations.

LEADER: In the desert, you gave the gifts of manna and of living water to the weary pilgrims whom you led by a cloud by day and a pillar of fire by night.

PEOPLE: At last, you sent your light into the world in the form of a tiny child, fragile and vulnerable, who grew to be the very Light of Light, full of grace and truth, revealing your glory on earth.

ALL: We thank you, O God, that you have sent Jesus Christ to bring life and immortality to light. Help us to receive your gifts with joy and humility: as we receive this bread and wine, may we open our hearts to receive your love and grace in Jesus Christ, and receive the love and support of one another. Be born among us, that we may give Christ's love to the world, through the presence and power of the Holy Spirit. Amen.

Words of Institution

Distribution of the Elements

Prayer of Thanksgiving

We give you thanks, O God, that you have come to us through Jesus Christ, both in the midst of time and history in the city of Bethlehem, and in the timeless presence of Christ's Spirit as we receive the gifts of bread and wine. Send us out into the world rejoicing, ready to share your love with the people we meet; through the grace of Jesus Christ. Amen.   (RAF/RCD)

G. *Statement for Presentation of Bibles to Young People on Bible Sunday*

—May this book be a constant reminder of a worthy past, a past torn and mended by peoples' dreams and ambitions, and by hope fulfilled in God's continuing love. This book carries a tremendous history, a history that is part of our identity as human beings, and part of who and what we are as the church. It is a history that gives meaning to our lives together. The biblical message can transform all of human history—past, present, and future.
—May this book enable you to dream today, and may your dreams challenge you to create a better tomorrow.
—May this book create within you a spirit of courage, responsibility, and hope. And may you become a bearer of its message of hope and love that overcome all.
—May the God of peace be with you always. Shalom and Amen.   (HWW)

H. *Benedictions*

1. (*Alludes to Luke 2:52*, RSV)
   LEADER: As Jesus grew in wisdom, so may you grow in faith and knowledge, in trust and truth.

PEOPLE: God grant that our understanding may increase and our witness grow stronger.

LEADER: As Christ knew God's presence and favor, so may you know your value and God's purpose for you.

PEOPLE: We accept ourselves as God's own children, as persons of worth and responsibility.

LEADER: As the babe of Bethlehem became the man of Nazareth, devoted to authentic sharing and caring, so may you become fully human, in God's image.

PEOPLE: We enter into Christ's service in another week and another year, open to new possibilities God may reveal to us.

LEADER: The peace of God go with you.

PEOPLE: And with you.

LEADER: Amen.

PEOPLE: Amen.

(LB)

2. Gabriel foretold it.
The angels heralded it.
The shepherds came to see for themselves.
And it is true. God is with us through Jesus Christ, the babe of Bethlehem and our resurrected Lord.
The world will never be the same; we ourselves will never be the same.
Go then and tell the world—Jesus Christ is born.

(PM)

I. Pastoral Prayers/Prayers for One Voice

1. *(Christmas Eve)*   God, you come to us and meet us in the strangest ways: sometimes in the stillness at the eye of the storm or in the midnight of our lives; sometimes in the raging whirlwind or in the high noon of our responsibilities; at times in the reflections of those who have lived long lives; at other times in the moment of birth when all is potential and the future cannot be known.

Meet us now as we remember the birth of the child Jesus who brought to Mary and Joseph the anxiety and joy of new life. When we, like Joseph, stand waiting, do not let us be frozen in inaction by a sense of futility because the future looks grim and out of control. When, like Mary, we ponder our lives, may our ideas of what you do never be so rigid that we mistake the work and teaching of your fool to be mere foolishness and insanity.

Arouse us from our habitual patterns of activities and send us like shepherds scurrying across the fields to some impossible birth of a new age because we have heard strange music in the wind praising God and announcing that God's greatest pleasure will be to give all creatures wholeness and peace.

Disturb our dreams of empires and dominions so that like the magi we may refuse to support the deceitful Herods of our day who promise status and national success sanctioned by religious piety and untroubled by prophetic judgment. While we mourn victims of war and poverty overseas, do not let us forget the slaughter of the innocents who in our own country die physically, emotion-

23

ally, and intellectually one by one because we have not imagined and enacted ways to bring peace to all.

And turn us into faithful dreamers who do not seek to return to our country or to some past era of our country by the same old ways, but who strike out for your country by another way.

Since you came and met those who celebrated the first Christmas, we are bold to seek your creating, redeeming, and sustaining presence here and now in one another and in what we have heard. Send us out into this dark night with new visions and dreams, with songs of thanksgiving and a new road to follow toward your realm. Amen.

(DRB)

2. *(Christmas)*   Eternal God, Ruler of all worlds and Shepherd of the stars, whose glory is revealed in vastness and in power, yet whose secret name is Love; this is the time when we remember your gentleness, hidden in a mother's hope and in the joy of a birth. This is the time when we believe again, if only for a season, that love is stronger than fear, peace more enduring than enmity, and that the darkness will never put out the light. And so, in this the season of midwinter spring, we offer to you the joy, the hopes, the dreams of children. We offer to you our gift of gratitude, and we make bold to believe that you have graced us with your presence, for we are gathered in the name of Love. Amen.

(DB)

3. *(First Sunday of the New Year)*
Now that the mad rush is over,
O center of stillness and peace:
Now that the needles are falling from the tree,
We thank you that you are still God-with-us.
As we face the year ahead,
help us to accept the difficult parts of our lives;
help us to make the changes we must make;
bring us to new places of openness and love toward you and the people around
     us;
help us to overcome the fears which keep us from fullness of life.
As the frigid days of January and February draw near
Help us to keep warm places alive within us,
where in secret
the bulbs of springtime tulips are nurtured.
As we face the year ahead,
we thank you for one another
and for your grace in Jesus Christ.
Help us individually and as a congregation
to be signs of your
compassion,
hope, joy, and unity
in this world you love in Jesus
our Christ. Amen.

(RCD)

Epiphany

A. Calls to Worship

(Paraphrases Isaiah 61:1–3, RSV; quotes Isaiah 60:1, RSV)
1. LEADER: Rejoice, for God has sent the Messiah
   PEOPLE: To bind up the brokenhearted,
   LEADER: To proclaim liberty to the captives,
   PEOPLE: To grant those who mourn a garland instead of ashes,
   LEADER: The mantle of praise, instead of a faint spirit.
   PEOPLE: Arise, shine, for our light has come.   (MSG)

2. LEADER: In the beginning our God created the light.
   PEOPLE: Morning broke open on the first day.
   LEADER: This God of ours sent the light.
   PEOPLE: Jesus the Christ came to the world's people.
   LEADER: Morning light opens for us.
   PEOPLE: God's Light illumines our lives; and opens us to worship this day.
                                                                     (BJW)

3. LEADER: As when Moses went up on the mountain and met you, O Mighty One—
   PEOPLE: We would make a covenant with you.
   LEADER: As when you sent the dove to light on Jesus' shoulder—
   PEOPLE: We would also carry your flame.
   LEADER: As when our Pilgrim forebears made their simple compact to live and walk with you—
   PEOPLE: So do we, in our own time, covenant, promise, to bear the burden of being your people.
   LEADER: Come, O God, and be among us!
   PEOPLE: Come, let us come close to God!   (RDS)

4. *(Sixth Sunday After Epiphany, Year A; paraphrases Psalm 119:33, 103, 105, 135, RSV)*
   LEADER: The word of God is a lamp to our feet and a light to our path.
   PEOPLE: God's word is sweet to the taste, sweeter than honey.
   LEADER: Teach us, O God, your holy way, for it is life to us.
   ALL: Accept our offerings of praise, O God. The earth is full of your steadfast love. Teach us your statutes! Amen.   (RCD)

5. *(Seventh Sunday After Epiphany, Year A; paraphrases the Sanctus and Psalm 29:2, KJV)*
   LEADER: Let us worship God in the beauty of holiness.
   PEOPLE: We worship the one God of all times and places, the Holy and Compassionate One.
   LEADER: We come trusting in God's grace to receive us, strange mixture of good and not-so-good that we are, individually and as a community.

ALL: Holy, holy, holy God: the world is full of your glory. We worship
         and praise you forever, world without end. Amen.   (RCD)

6. Call to Awareness   *(Alludes to Ezekiel 37:1–14, RSV)*

Our joints were connected
by Christ's coming.
The promise
of no more dislocation
but collection and fixation.
Everybody knows
God gathered up the bones
and Ezekiel danced in the valley
with the clattering recollection—
God dance,
bone dance.
The body knows
how well it's put together.
The body knows
Jesus was a human
who called his bones
to come,
and dance together.   (WUMC)

B. Unison Prayers

1. *(Alludes to Matthew 2:1–12, RSV)*   God of all people and all places, like the
magi we would journey into the presence of Jesus the Christ. There we would
offer our gifts; before Christ, we would lay the realities of our lives, good and
bad. We offer our joy and love and laughter, that they might be made holy; we
relinquish our bitterness and hatred and worry, that we might be made whole
once more; through the living Spirit of Christ. Amen.   (RCD)

2. *(Alludes to Psalm 119:105, RSV)*   God of light, whose presence shines before us as a lamp unto our feet, and whose brilliance overpowers the darkness of
this sad and tormented world; shine in our hearts as evening descends, that we
may look into the future and discern in the shadows the form of your Christ,
whose kindly light leads us on. This we pray in the name of Christ who is the
light of the world. Amen.   (RWD)

3. *(Alludes to John 2:1–11, RSV)*   Great God of the old and the new, take our
lives and make them like new wine. Refresh our spirits. Disturb our apathy.
Strengthen us with your courage. For we seek to be new people, and your presence gives us joy. Be with us as we worship, and as we go from this place in
work and play. Through Christ with us. Amen.   (SEG)

4. Living Christ, your earthly ministry was full of struggle as well as joy; yet
you were faithful in following God's will. Breathe your Spirit into our lives, that

we may never fall back from the way of discipleship or the effort of loving. Grant that we may find true joy and peace as we accept the cost of faithful discipleship. For it is in your name we pray. Amen. (SEG)

5. (*Alludes to John 15:1–11*, RSV)   In the dark winter days when we often get discouraged, we turn, O God, to you. Teach us to abide in Christ, that we may know the joy you intend for your people. As branches attached to the vine of your love, may love and goodness grow within us, through the power of the Counselor, the Holy Spirit. Amen. (RCD)

6. (*Second Sunday After Epiphany, Year C; alludes to 1 Corinthians 12:4–11*, RSV)   O God, Eternal Spirit, you have empowered the faithful of past ages to preach and to heal. We pray that you would be known among us in power as well, bestowing your gifts, that we might carry out your mission in unity and in peace; through the grace of Jesus Christ. Amen. (RCD)

7. (*Sixth Sunday After Epiphany, Year A*)   We thank you, Holy God, for the vision of faithful life lifted up by Jesus; yet we live in a world where divorce is common and oaths are taken lightly. Give those of us who are married the wisdom and courage to live in faithfulness. Look kindly on us in our weakness, when we fail. Free us from self-righteousness, when we see others fail. May your church be a place where life-giving relationships are supported and nurtured; through the grace of Jesus Christ. Amen. (RCD)

8. (*Ninth Sunday After Epiphany, Year A; alludes to Ezekiel 34 and Matthew 25:31–49*, RSV)   Tender shepherd of our lives, we give you thanks that you seek us and gather us together as your people. We give thanks that we can feed on your love, and that you count us among the sheep of your pasture. As you feed us, may we feed those who hunger for food, for life, for understanding, and for justice. So may others know you through knowing us. In the name of Jesus we pray. Amen. (RCD)

C. Prayer of Confession

(*Seventh Sunday After Epiphany, Year A*)   Sometimes, O God, your word is too much for us. You ask us to love our enemies, when we can scarcely love our friends as we should. You ask us to give when we want to take, and to forgive when we want to nurse bitterness. We thank you that you accept us as we are, and that you show us what we can be. Help us to believe that we can be loving, just, and holy like you; through the grace of Jesus Christ. Amen. (RCD)

D. The Corporate Confession

LEADER: The Light comes to the world:
PEOPLE: Our eyes, long used to darkness,
　　　　　Fatigued from long searching,

Blink and twitch.
We jerk away and do not answer.
LEADER: The Light comes to our lives:
PEOPLE: Shuddering with the warmth,
Preferring loneliness to the pain
Of answering,
We jerk away and do not answer.
LEADER: The Light comes to touch our bodies
And our spirit-minds:
PEOPLE: But we are lost in logic,
Living in our heads.
Our bodies give us away
To the truth of isolation.
LEADER: Calling, calling our names,
The Light comes:
PEOPLE: Preferring to hear it as
The ice-rattling branches of
Winter trees
We turn away,
Crouched against the wind,
And do not answer.
(Moment of silence)

Words of Assurance

We have seen the Light.
We have heard the call.
We will dance in the Light
With our God.

The Benediction

The Light has splintered our darkness.
God has called us to dance.
We go forth to answer with our lives.   (WUMC)

E. Affirmation of Faith

(Based on Isaiah 60:1–2 and John 1:1–14, RSV)

LEADER: The star of divine promise shines before us still.
PEOPLE: Over a world of mute hopes, dim visions, dark fears, still the light
shines.
LEADER: In a world shrouded by darkness both tragic and willful,
PEOPLE: Still we proclaim:
Our light has come.
The glory of God shines upon us.

LEADER: For One born of God is born of our own flesh, and that One is light for our lives.

PEOPLE: As we receive the light and let it shine through us, it rises as a beacon for a darkened world.

LEADER: The peoples shall stream toward its promise; meek and mighty alike share in its dawning brightness.

PEOPLE: Then all shall say:
Arise! The glory of God is upon us! (MLP)

Lent

A. A Journey to the Edge

Call to Awareness

LEADER: Lent calls us to journey along the edge, to anticipate that final trip to Jerusalem.

PEOPLE: Lent calls us to the cutting edge, when the wheat falls to the ground and new life comes forth; the cutting of a new covenant.

LEADER: Lent calls us not only to give up something, but also to take upon ourselves as community the intention of true participation in the mystery of God-with-us.

PEOPLE: Lent calls us to corporate penitence, accountability, and preparation.

LEADER: Lent calls us to concentrate upon our baptismal vocation to be a sign of the New Earth.

PEOPLE: Lent calls us to face the darkness without holding a flashlight.

Unison Prayer of Confession

We do not always walk well along the edge, God.
At times we fall into chasms which separate us from you, from one another, from ourselves.
With eyes closed, we risk falling into the abyss.
We attempt to stabilize our journey by demanding signs and seeking wisdom along the way.
We fail to ask, "Where is Christ being sacrificed now?"
At the end of our journey the hour will be at hand.
The questions flood our conscious minds:
What would we have done that night in Gethsemane?
Could we have been part of the political machinery that murdered Christ?
We shudder at the answers.
We need the strength and assurance of your grace.
(A few moments of silent prayer)

Words of Assurance   (*In unison; paraphrases Romans 8:38–39*, RSV)

We have this assurance that neither death, nor life, nor angels, nor principalities, nor things present, nor things to come, nor powers, nor height, nor depth, nor anything else in all creation, will be able to separate us from the love of God in Jesus Christ. Amen.   (WUMC)

B. Calls to Worship

1. LEADER: In this season, we worship remembering Jesus' death in love for us and all people.
    PEOPLE: Lent is a time of tears.
    LEADER: But out of tears, joy is born—the joy of sin forgiven, hope reborn, and life restored.
    ALL: We stand in awe of the God who brings joy out of tears, and life out of death. Let us worship with reverence. Amen.   (RCD)

2. (*Quotes Ecclesiastes 3:1–2, 6*, RSV)
    LEADER: For everything there is a season,
    PEOPLE: And a time for every matter under heaven:
    LEADER: A time to be born,
    PEOPLE: And a time to die;
    LEADER: A time to keep,
    PEOPLE: And a time to give away.
    LEADER: This is the season for repentance,
    PEOPLE: For turning away from aimlessness and sin;
    LEADER: For re-turning our lives to God,
    PEOPLE: As joyful disciples of Christ.   (MSG)

3. (*Second Sunday in Lent, Year A*)
    LEADER: We gather as pilgrims on a journey of faith.
    PEOPLE: We come seeking the awareness of God's presence as we travel on.
    LEADER: We come seeking light for our darkness, strength in our weakness.
    ALL: Shine in our hearts, O God, with the light of your love. Make your presence known through Jesus the Christ. Amen.   (RCD)

4. (*Third Sunday in Lent, Year C; alludes to Exodus 3:1–15*, RSV)
    LEADER: Come to this time of worship in reverent awe.
    PEOPLE: The place where we are standing is holy ground.
    LEADER: Know the presence and power of the Living God.
    PEOPLE: God comes to us as a burning fire that does not consume, a revelation bringing warmth and vitality.
    LEADER: We have known God throughout our history.
    PEOPLE: Yet there is so much of God we do not know. God's purposes are so far beyond our understanding.
    LEADER: Now in these moments we would be open to the unexpected.

PEOPLE: Come, Holy Spirit, that we may respond. Discipline and cultivate us, that our lives may bear fruit. (LB)

5. (*Quotes Psalm 119:105; alludes to Exodus 16:4–21; 17:1–7; paraphrases Ephesians 3:21;* RSV)
LEADER: We are on a journey of faith.
PEOPLE: We travel with Jesus Christ as our guide.
LEADER: The promises of God shine like a star before us and give us strength for the journey;
PEOPLE: But still, in the wilderness, we become impatient and rebellious, and lose our way.
LEADER: We gather, seeking to be fed by the manna of God's Word, to rediscover the paths of righteousness.
ALL: O God, your Word is a lamp to our feet and a light to our path. Glory be to you in Jesus Christ and in the church to all generations. Amen. (RCD)

6. LEADER: From the wanderings of our lives, we have come to gather here.
PEOPLE: We bring life with us, to this time and place.
LEADER: Come here, offering your lives before God,
PEOPLE: And the presence of God will go with us and remain with us in our play and work, in our resting and our service. (SEG)

7. (*Alludes to the hymn "Now Thank We All Our God"*)
LEADER: We have gathered in the presence of God, who is love.
PEOPLE: We have gathered in the shadow of the cross, sign of God's love.
LEADER: Let us give thanks for the compassion of God, the grace of Jesus Christ, and the unity of the Holy Spirit.
ALL: We will pray and sing, praising God with hearts and hands and voices. Amen. (RCD)

8. (*Paraphrases Dietrich Bonhoeffer,* The Cost of Discipleship, *trans. R.H. Fuller [New York: Macmillan Co., 1959], p. 79*)
LEADER: We follow Christ
PEOPLE: Who says, "Take up your cross."
LEADER: We follow Christ
PEOPLE: Who bids us come and die.
LEADER: We follow Christ
PEOPLE: Who summons us to *new* life.
LEADER: Come, let us worship our Creator. (MSG)

C. Unison Prayers

1. (*First Sunday in Lent, Year A; alludes to Genesis 2:4–8,* RSV)   Creator God, it is you who have made us, and not we ourselves. We are dust without your breath of life. We are creatures, not Creator; yet you entrust the care of creation

to us. Breathe your Spirit into us that we might be faithful in the tasks you set before us; through Jesus Christ, who came to redeem your lost creation. Amen.   (RCD)

2. (*Second Sunday in Lent, Year A; paraphrases Psalm 119:105*, RSV)
Abraham and Sarah went out, not knowing where they were headed, because they trusted in you. Jesus went forward to his death in Jerusalem, trusting in your purpose. Help us, like them, to take you at your word, and thus to move onward in faith. Be the lamp to our feet, and the light to our path, through your Spirit of life and wisdom. Amen.   (RCD)

3. (*Transfiguration; Second Sunday in Lent, Year C*)   Gracious God, we thank you for the glimpses of your glory, and the whispered words of your promise, which help us to continue from day to day. Help us to press onward in the journey of faith, trusting your grace for today and tomorrow, accepting the cost and joy of discipleship to Jesus Christ our faithful guide. Amen.
                                                                                           (RCD)

4. God most compassionate and merciful, we thank you that you have come to us in Jesus the Servant-Christ, whose disciples we are. Make us strong in your strength; make us wise in your wisdom; and make us gentle in your compassion. May we be signs of the human unity you seek to accomplish through the cross of Jesus Christ, that your name may be glorified in all the earth. Amen.
                                                                                           (RCD)

D. Confession

1. Call to Confession

Standing beneath the cross of Jesus, as we observe the season of Lent, is a sobering experience, for the cross judges both our world and our individual lives.
       Today, people are still crucified by the same forces that destroyed Jesus. Today, each of us falls short of the resolve and dedication to God which Jesus exhibited by the way he lived and died.
       So let us, as men and women who live in a twisted world and who are all too weak in spirit, join together in the prayer of confession.   (RNE)

2. Prayer of Confession

We surround ourselves with crosses, O God; yet we confess that we shrink back from the awareness that your glory is revealed in the criminal's cross of Jesus Christ. Help us to know your presence wherever there is suffering in our world; may we be channels of your love and healing, so that you may not suffer needlessly. We pray these things in the name of Jesus Christ. Amen.   (RCD)

3. (*Alludes to Exodus 17:1–7*, RSV)   Gracious God, we acknowledge that when the going gets rough, we begin to assert ourselves and our own needs, and we pull back from community. Like the Israelites in the desert, we murmur and complain; we criticize and blame. In your compassion, forgive us; help us,

through the grace of Jesus Christ, to maintain our unity of purpose and commitment even in the wilderness days. For it is in Christ's name that we pray. Amen. (RCD)

4. Assurance *(Fourth Sunday in Lent, Year B; paraphrases Ephesians 2:14, RSV)*

LEADER: Through Christ, the dividing walls have been broken down.
PEOPLE: We have been handed the hope that we can live our lives in new ways.
LEADER: Such a gift surely sets us free!
PEOPLE: We are free! And we will rise as God's freely chosen ones, shining forth in the world with love! (RCD)

5. Call to Confession *(Fifth Sunday in Lent, Year A; alludes to Ezekiel 37:11–14, RSV)*

As we consider the dry bones of Ezekiel's vision, we realize that sometimes we are dry, lifeless, despairing in our Christian faith and practice. Let us pray.

Prayer of Confession

Spirit and Breath of Life, before you we recognize that our spirits are not fully alive. We have succumbed to the sin of despair; we have been lifeless, not lively, in our faith. Like dry bones, we are brittle and break under pressure. Breathe your Spirit of power into us, that our faith may be active, in word and deed, and that your name may be glorified in Jesus, our Christ. Amen.

Words of Assurance

The good news is that we depend not on ourselves, but on the Spirit of God to give us vitality. Thanks be to God. Amen. (RCD)

6. Litany of Confession

LEADER: In Jesus Christ, God came among us to save us from sin and death. In walking to the cross, Christ freed us from bondage of guilt and judgment. We come before God now, seeking grace freely given.
PEOPLE: Grant us your grace, O God, and free us.
LEADER: When we hear and obey the voice of the world rather than turning to you for guidance—
PEOPLE: Grant us your grace, O God, and free us.
LEADER: When we critically judge others without wanting to look at ourselves—
PEOPLE: Grant us your grace, O God, and free us.
LEADER: When we fail to love any of your people out of prejudice and fear—
PEOPLE: Grant us your grace, O God, and free us.

Silent Confession

Assurance of Forgiveness

LEADER: In the cross, we see God's amazing love for us. We are God's children living in a confused world. So in abundant grace, God answers our doubt, heals our pain, and forgives our failures in grace. I announce therefore in the name of Jesus Christ, we are forgiven and made new.

PEOPLE: In the name of Jesus Christ, we are forgiven and set free in grace. Thanks be to God forever more! Amen. (JCW)

E. Collects Before the Scriptures

1. *(Second Sunday in Lent, Year C)* Your blessings, poured out into our lives, are more numerous than the stars. When we hear your word aright, we are sometimes dazzled by the brightness of new insights. Open us to fresh thoughts; then move us beyond mere thinking to appropriate action. In Christ we pray. Amen. (LB)

2. *(Third Sunday in Lent, Year C)* We await your Word, holy God, in the words of others who have walked with you and now share their story with us. On mountaintops of aspiration and low valleys of despair, they have sensed a presence they had no words to describe. Yet they used these symbols to reach for a truth that was beyond them. May we hear all you would have us hear, both warning and reassurance, both judgment and promise. Amen. (LB)

3. *(Fourth Sunday in Lent, Year C)* Nourish us, O God, with your word of life. Bring us to our senses so your purposes may be apparent to us. Take away both the uncertainty and the arrogance in our views of ourselves. We would rejoice with our sisters and brothers who are finding new life. Grant that we may hear your music and be freed to join in the dancing. Amen. (LB)

4. *(Maundy Thursday, Year C)* Eternal God, link us now with our ancestors in the faith, that their experience and the traditions built around them may move us to new sincerity of conviction and purpose. Prepare us for the trials we may yet face, empowering us with your truth and the courage to claim it in our darkest hours. Amen. (LB)

F. Resources for Palm Sunday

1. Litany *(Paraphrases Luke 19:38, RSV)*
  LEADER: The winds of God blow strong and compelling through the stagnant atmosphere of our neglect.
  PEOPLE: We feel the insistent warmth of God's presence and seek to awaken from our lethargy.
  LEADER: God invites us to join the parade of the faithful, to demonstrate for justice, truth, and righteousness.
  PEOPLE: We are drawn to the pageantry of Palm Sunday and to the One who comes in life-changing peace.
  LEADER: Whatever our state of mind or condition of life, we are welcomed to this time of self-searching and worship.

PEOPLE: Blessed is the one who comes in God's name. Peace in heaven and glory in the highest!

LEADER: Amen.

PEOPLE: Amen. (LB)

2. Unison Prayer

Living God, you give us this day, full of hope and promise. As our ancestors waved palms in praise of Christ, we bring our praises, too, that in joy you may take our lives and transform us as your ministers alive. Through Jesus Christ we pray. Amen. (SEG)

3. Confession   (*Alludes to Luke 19:40*, RSV)

Call to Confession

The choice is ever before us: discipleship or rejection, authentic response or play-acting, commitment that will go all the way to a cross or hypocrisy which is a living denial and death. Like the fickle crowds of the first Palm Sunday, we need to examine ourselves and question the genuineness of our commitment.

Confession of Sin

God of all times and places, we confess that we would rather join the crowds than stand alone. We prefer the popular point of view to a solitary witness for justice and truth. We like safety and security while shrinking from the risk of involvement. We'll sing "hosanna" when everyone else is doing so—but not when the hostile "Good Friday" forces may hear us. We do not like to admit our lukewarm response to you, but neither do we want to be considered fanatics.

We believe Jesus Christ came into the world to save sinners. We know that means us, not just other folk involved in obvious evils everyone knows about. We ask you to be patient with us, to help us understand our own guilt. Then pour out your forgiveness in such a way that we are forever transformed. In Jesus' name. Amen.

Assurance of Forgiveness

God sweeps into our human scene, redeeming all who turn from evil and do good. There is grace, mercy, and renewed strength for all who earnestly seek the new life Christ brings. Let us rejoice together, for even the stones cry out with good news. God forgives. We are freed from the burden of our sin. Praise God! (LB)

4. Benediction   (*Alludes to Matthew 21:9*, RSV)

LEADER: When you leave this gathering, sing hosannas. Carry their glad cry into this new week.

PEOPLE: However popular or unpopular the cause, we wish to follow Jesus Christ.

LEADER: God overlooks our past and sends us into the world as representatives of the good news.

PEOPLE: God in Christ is bringing wholeness to our lives and giving us opportunities to minister to others.

LEADER: We have been commissioned and empowered to make a difference in the quality of life around us.

PEOPLE: Hosanna! Blessed are all who go forth to serve. Glory to God in the highest! (LB)

G. Maundy Thursday Call to Worship

(*Based on portions of Psalm 27*, RSV)

LEADER: God is my light and my salvation: whom shall I fear?

PEOPLE: God is the strength of my life: whom shall I dread?

LEADER: Your presence, O God, I am seeking.

PEOPLE: Abandon me not to my foes, for deceivers rise up to oppose me, breathing out violence.

LEADER: Trust in God. Stand fast and strengthen your courage.

ALL: Do not leave me or forsake me, O God, my salvation! (RCD)

H. Resources for Good Friday

1. Call to Worship (*Good Friday, Year C; paraphrases Isaiah 53:5*, RSV)

LEADER: Fear and fascination drew observers to the first Holy Friday. These emotions have attracted people ever since.

PEOPLE: We cannot flee from the pain and suffering which Jesus experienced on our behalf.

LEADER: We wonder why one so faithful and loving had to face the agony of rejection and death.

PEOPLE: Jesus was wounded for our transgressions, and was bruised for our iniquities.

LEADER: In this time of worship we join Christ at Calvary, aware of our involvement in the cruelty there.

PEOPLE: Our faithfulness is tested at the cross and our lives are judged by our response. (LB)

2. Confession (*Alludes to Revelation 7:9 and Psalm 23:4*, RSV)

Call to Confession

Good Friday is not a day of safe distances. The darkness descends. Taunts and jeers reach our ears when we dare to identify with the Light of the World. We who are called the body of Christ in today's world, drawn from every tribe, language, nation, and race, have come to our time of testing. The world God loves resists our witness for shalom as it rejected the Christ. Will we go all the way to the cross?

Prayer of Confession

God of the hilltops and of low places, Revealer at Sinai and Reassuring One in the valley of the shadow of death, we need you here. You have created us and given life to all things, but we have chased after other gods and ridiculed those who practice their faith too seriously. We have tried to put you to the test, but have not wanted to be tested ourselves. We place conditions on our belief and limit our trust while the One you sent to love us is rejected, tortured, and killed. O God, what have we done? Is it too late to be a disciple? Hear our cry! Amen.

Assurance of Forgiveness

God's love is not destroyed at Golgotha, nor diminished by our unclear reflection of its saving power. God reaches out to heal and revive us, and to reveal again the love that will not let us go. We are invited to know the One beyond all knowing and to accept the gifts God offers us. Answer God's love with your praise, devotion, and service—and you will know you are forgiven.   (LB)

3. Benediction   *(Abridges Revelation 5:12, RSV)*

LEADER: Go out to keep your vigil at the cross. Let prayer and meditation be a means of transformation.

PEOPLE: We carry with us the tragedy of this day. But also its possibilities for reclaiming a heritage and recovering a faith to sustain and move us.

LEADER: Share the agony of Jesus' rejection and death, knowing how often we add to the pain.

PEOPLE: Our intent is to "take up our cross and follow." But we shrink from the anguish and falter at the cost.

LEADER: Say "yes" to the Christ, without excuses or reservations.

PEOPLE: Worthy is the One who was slain, to receive glory and honor and power.   (LB)

4. Call to Confession

LEADER: Judas, slave of jealousy, where are you?

PEOPLE: I am here.

LEADER: Peter, slave of fear, where are you?

PEOPLE: I am here.

LEADER: Thomas, slave of doubt, where are you?

PEOPLE: I am here.

LEADER: Men and women of Jerusalem, enslaved to mob rule, where are you?

PEOPLE: I am here.

LEADER: Pilate, slave of expediency, where are you?

PEOPLE: I am here.

LEADER: The story of Christ's passion and death mirrors for us much of our own weakness and sin. We all come *here* as men and women who have missed the mark and who are alienated from God and our neighbor near and far. Let us join together in the prayer of confession.

(RNE)

5. Prayer of Confession

Yes, dear God, it's true. We are not worthy of your love. We promise to be faithful but we fall away; we forsake you; we flee from you; we betray you; we deny you; we watch from afar; we don't tell anyone that your reign is at hand; we are afraid. Change us, we pray. Amen. (MLS)

6. An Affirmation and Prayer for Good Friday *(Alludes to Romans 8:22 and Philippians 2:10–11, RSV)*

Our God,
Is this your son Jesus hanging on the cross?
The one who healed the sick, taught us how to live in your ways, proclaimed the
    coming of your reign?
The one who was to share fully in your glory and sovereign rule?
Is it through this dying one,
    is it from this cross that you assert your reign?
So this is where you reign.
You, Giver of Life, suffering, renewing, claiming dominion
Here, where the power of death would force its way:

Here at this hospital bed,
    where someone is dying of cancer.

Here amidst the wreckage of the accident,
    where children, their frames crushed, struggle to live.

Here in the welfare office,
    where those who wait are measuring their hopes.

Here in these tents,
    where refugees mourn for homes they have fled.

Here in this world,
    wherever death stalks your children:
This is where you reign.

Give light to our vision, O God,
that we may discover you, our Creator,
    amidst this groaning creation.
Stir faith in our hearts,
that our tongues may sing and knees bend
    before the exalted One who suffers.
Give strength to our love,
that where life struggles to prevail,
    we would bring your renewing Spirit.
We pray, as we would live,
    in the name of that One whose power is shaped as a cross:
    Jesus, our Christ. Amen.

(Note from author: In our Good Friday service, I prayed the first and last sections alone. The phrases beginning "Here . . ." were read by five persons, each of whom rose in place to pray his or her section and remained standing to the end of the prayer.) (MLP)

Easter

A. *Calls to Worship for Easter Sunday and Season*

1. LEADER: Easter is—
   PEOPLE: Chocolate rabbits, fuzzy yellow chicks and vacation!
   LEADER: Easter is—
   PEOPLE: Joy, life renewing, and a renewal of faith and spirit!
   LEADER: Easter is—
   PEOPLE: The great turning point, a risen One, a celebration in Christ!
   LEADER: Sunrise is—
   PEOPLE: Beautiful! The end of darkness! The beginning of new life!
   LEADER: Hope is—
   PEOPLE: What makes the world go round; a way into the future; a light at the end of a dark spiritual tunnel.
   LEADER: Hope is—
   PEOPLE: A new friendship; getting free from fear; what keeps us going.
   LEADER: Hope is—
   PEOPLE: In Christ's victory—the end of despair! Amen.   (JHY)

2. LEADER: Christ has risen.
   PEOPLE: Christ has risen indeed.
   LEFT: God is alive . . .
   RIGHT: New birth is given.
   LEFT: Hope is alive . . .
   RIGHT: A new age is dawning.
   LEFT: Joy is alive . . .
   RIGHT: Redemption is here.
   LEFT: Love is alive . . .
   RIGHT: Death cannot harm us.
   LEFT: We are alive . . .
   RIGHT: New life is within us.
   LEFT: The church is alive . . .
   RIGHT: God's Spirit is within us.
   ALL: God of life, we worship you.
   God of creation, we praise you.
   God of revelation, we learn from you.
   God of resurrection, we are here to celebrate you.   (WUMC)

3. LEADER: Welcome to God's new day!
   PEOPLE: Everywhere we look we see new life!
   LEADER: In seeds and buds, in smiles and touch, we discover God's energizing presence.
   PEOPLE: Death can never be the last word.
   LEADER: God has raised Jesus Christ from the dead. Christ is present among us today.
   ALL: Praise God for new life within and among us this day! Amen.

   (LB)

4. The tomb, death's stone-cold womb, could not contain him, God's offspring, life's child.
   The tomb, Easter's empty surprise, brimmed full of meaning as death itself passed away.
   The women, Easter's unlikely reporters, told of a gaping void within the gravestone that filled their emptiness with joy.
   The women, discoverers afraid and amazed, proclaimed, "He is risen!" and were told by slow believers to hush their idle chatter.
   The event, God's Son-rise, enlightened a dark earth as Jesus's return brought dawn to a new day.
   The event, impossibility made possible, dazzles our eyes yet clears our vision.
   We see the empty cross, the tomb, and we toss back our heads and laugh for joy. We gather to worship the God who gives us Easter.   (GER)

5. LEADER: Alleluia! Praise be to God! Christ has risen indeed.
   PEOPLE: We bring our joyful alleluias to this place today!
   LEADER: The tomb is empty, and new life hovers in this dawn.
   PEOPLE: We praise God for the mystery and the excitement of new life present in this day!
   (SEG)

6. Last Sunday was Easter, a day on which the only fitting call to worship was announcement of the Event—the resurrection, the greatest act of life-saving imaginable. Through it God let us laugh at our death sentence by punctuating it with a living exclamation mark. On this day and in days to come may we remember that there are times when God restates the joyful resurrection proclamation.

   Abilities faded and forgotten are channeled toward new creativity—that's resurrection.

   Friendships once killed by frosty misunderstanding bloom again in warm reconciliation—that's resurrection.

   Hopes glimmering and gone are rekindled by expressions of caring—that's resurrection.

   Faith, dulled by lack of exercise, dances again to God's everyday rhythms—that's resurrection.

   We worship the God whose resurrecting power lives on as does the Christ we serve.
   (GER)

7. LEADER: Today is a new day!
   PEOPLE: New life is rising among us!
   LEADER: Today we are challenged to live fully in God's love!
   PEOPLE: So we will greet one another in love and praise the God who uplifts each of us in grace!
   ALL: Alleluia! Amen! (SEG)

8. LEADER: Today is a new day! *3-30-97*
   PEOPLE: We come with the past behind us, and the future open. We come to celebrate the new life Christ brings.
   LEADER: Christ is with us! *He lives!*
   PEOPLE: Christ is with us indeed! *He lives with us forever!* (SEG)

9. (*Third Sunday in Eastertide, Year A; paraphrases Luke 24:35 and Acts 17:28, RSV*)
   LEADER: The disciples met the risen Christ as they went about their daily tasks—eating, fishing, preparing a meal.
   PEOPLE: We have gathered because we too want to know the presence of Jesus among us.
   LEADER: We gather around his table to know him in the breaking of bread.
   PEOPLE: We will return to the world, seeking to know and to make known his presence there.
   ALL: Glory be to God, Creator, Christ, and Spirit of life, in whom we live and move and have our being. Amen. (RCD)

B. Invocation for Easter Sunday *3-30-97 (adapted)*

Dear God, this past week has been one of mixed emotions; of faith struggling to understand. We have greeted you with palm branches; we have sat at table with you to share a farewell meal. We have witnessed your death on a simple wooden cross. Yet on the third day, you come to us again in victory. By this, we know that death is not the final word. As the sun boldly rises to meet a new day, rise in our lives this Easter morning, for you are our hope, our life, and our joy. Amen. (KCHS)

C. Unison Prayers for Easter Sunday and Season

1. God of all ages and of all people, the shadows and gloom of Good Friday have been dispersed by the light and color of Easter Sunday. We rejoice in your power that turns our sorrow into joy, our despair into hope, our defeat into victory and evil into goodness. Help us on this Easter morning, O God, to burst out of the tombs that have trapped us: tombs of selfishness and sinfulness, greed and gluttony, scandal and corruption, pride and prejudice. Let now a new life of divine grace and human love burst forth from each of us this Easter day, through the grace of Jesus Christ, the Risen One. Amen. (RHM)

2. (*Second Sunday in Eastertide, Year A; alludes to Hebrews 10:31; 1 Peter 1:3–9; and Isaiah 40:12;* RSV) What an awe-inspiring thing it is, O God, to fall into your hands: to be shaped like clay, to be forged through the fire of suffering and conflict! Grant that we might rejoice in your work within and among us, and that we might find our home in the hollow of your hand, through Jesus our Risen Christ, to whom be praise and honor and glory forever. Amen.

(RCD)

3. (*Third Sunday in Eastertide, Year A; alludes to Psalm 90:6,* RSV) We thank you, O God, that you have given us new life and freedom in Jesus Christ. Our faith and our hope are in you. Since our earthly lives pass like the flowers of the field, which bloom today and fade tomorrow, we want to be rooted securely in your eternal love. Be known to us as we live from day to day, through the grace of Jesus Christ. Amen.

(RCD)

4. (*Sixth Sunday in Eastertide, Year C; alludes to Luke 19:42 and Revelation 7:9–12; 22:1–5;* RSV) We pray to you, O God, for the life of our city, that its leaders and people might learn the things that make for peace. We thank you for the vision of a city centered on your worship and service, where diverse people live in harmony. Through the grace of Jesus Christ, may we share in making our earthly city more like that heavenly city. Amen.

(RCD)

D. Confessions—Easter Season

1. Dear God, Creator of the heavens and Maker of each small thing: what a wondrous universe you have spread before us. Each day overflows with the richness of life: with growing green and bursting blossoms, with relationships which nurture and challenge, with missions accomplished and justice to be done. Each day is full of your meaning. And yet many times we do not see this. With much around us to be done, we complain of boredom. Or we are so busy we lose track of your presence and calling. Too often we scurry to and fro without appreciation, delight, or much sense of purpose. Call us, O God, out of emotional poverty into the richness of life lived in love. Move us toward you and one another. Amen.

(LME)

2. The Corporate Confession (*in unison*)

O God, we confess our lack of faith. Although we have called you the God of hope, we often feel lost, cynical, without hope. The world is so full of big nails and little nails—people are put on so many different kinds of crosses in so many different places that we wonder if there can ever be enough resurrections. We are reluctant to leave the tomb of our own ignorance and fear to claim the promise.

We confess that our weaknesses and insensitivities stand in the way of new life in our world. We know that the world is full of suffering. Our brothers and sisters are nailed to crosses of poverty and injustice. People close enough to touch are sealed in tombs of loneliness and despair. But we have failed to halt the crucifixion, to roll away the stone.

Words of Assurance

Our confession is an acknowledgment of our humanness, our need for God's grace. God has promised that we can be forgiven for our weaknesses, our insensitivities, our cynicism and our lack of faith. We accept this assurance with humility and with the hope that it will lead us toward resurrection.

(WUMC)

E. Collect Before the Scriptures *(Easter Sunday, Year C)*

Holy and powerful God, as far beyond our comprehension as is the grand design of your universe, we seek to know you through the poor vehicle of words. May we go beyond hearing to doing. Grant that we may feel your presence, as did the followers who knew Jesus in the breaking of bread. May we experience the fire within that sent them out to share good news. Amen. (LB)

F. Litany for Easter Sunday

LEADER: Trembling, the women approached the tomb. The tomb: that mysterious place of meeting. Death meeting life. Women meeting the risen Christ. Trembling.

PEOPLE: Trembling, we approach the edge where death and life meet. Death, the unknown, meets life, new life. New life faces us with its possibilities and uncertainties. Trembling, we approach.

LEADER: Easter morning: the women came face to face with Jesus, face to face with the risen Christ. They doubted, they feared, they wondered as life returned to them from death.

PEOPLE: From a triumphant Palm Sunday to a dark, betrayed Friday, we have journeyed to Easter. Wiser now, we know that joy and sorrow, life and death are bound together. Passing through sorrow, through death, to life and joy, we arrive at Easter.

LEADER: The risen Jesus still bore the marks of the nails. Life knows death, joy knows sorrow. Yet it is life which triumphs over all the love which conquers all threats.

PEOPLE: Death is shattered. Face to face, the disciples saw death had lost its power.

LEADER: We have survived the deaths, the sorrows, the pains. We receive new life.

PEOPLE: Rejoice! Life bursts through death. God is with us. Alleluia!

(SRH)

G. Offering Prayer for Easter

Wonderful, amazing, God, we thank you that you have raised Jesus Christ from the dead, bringing us the promise of new life. With the dawning of this new day, may we awake to new opportunities to love and serve you and witness to Christ whom you have raised. Use us, and our gifts, to your glory. In Jesus' name we pray. Amen. (RCD)

H. Benediction for Easter

Burst forth from the cocoons which enslave you!
Fly free as the butterfly.
Shine bright as the rainbow.
Christ has risen!
Go in peace.
Go in joy.
Amen. (SRH)

Resources for the Festival of the Christian Home

A. Calls to Worship

1. (*Paraphrases Ephesians 3:15–21,* RSV)
   LEADER: We gather in the presence of God, through whom all families on earth receive their life and their name.
   PEOPLE: We wish to be strengthened in our inner selves, that Christ may dwell in our hearts.
   LEADER: We seek to be rooted and grounded in God's love and in the love of Christ which surpasses understanding.
   PEOPLE: We come to worship and to praise the source of love and peace.
   ALL: Glory be to God in the church and in Jesus Christ to all generations forever and ever. Amen. (RCD)

2. (*Peace and Family Life; paraphrases Ephesians 3:15,* RSV)
   LEADER: We have gathered in the presence of the God in whom every family in heaven and on earth receives its name.
   PEOPLE: We come, in the prayer that the peace of Christ might dwell in our family relationships.
   LEADER: We come, in the prayer that the peace of God might permeate the life of the human family.
   ALL: May the love of Christ fill our hearts, our lives, and our world, to the glory of God. Amen. (RCD)

B. Collect

(Paraphrases the invocation in the 1968 UCC Order for Marriage)
Gracious God, we your children praise you for all the gifts of your grace. We thank you for those who are our partners in the adventure of living; we thank you for Jesus Christ, who in serving love gave all human partnerships new meaning. And since without your help we can do nothing as we ought, we pray you to enrich us with your grace, that we may be faithful and loving in all our relationships; through the Spirit of Jesus the Christ. Amen.   (RCD)

C. Prayers of Confession

1. Loving God, we realize that we have not made our homes the dwelling place for your love that we would like. Too often, we act like individuals who happen to share the same building, rather than family members who care for one another. Help us to renew our commitments to the growth and development of those who share our homes with us. Help us to communicate openly with one another and to show our love in the homes where we live. Amen.   (SRH)

2. *(Peace and Family Life)*   God of peace and justice, we long for the peace within, and without. We long to find serenity of spirit in the midst of life's struggles. We long for harmony in our families and in all our relationships. We long for the day when each family everywhere might live in peace without fear, enjoying the fruit of vine and tree. Yet we confess that there is much anxiety, fear, distrust, and even violence within us. We are not willing to take the risks and make the sacrifices which peace requires. Look upon us with kindness and mercy; rule in our hearts and our world; and show us how to walk in your paths; through the grace of Jesus Christ. Amen.   (RCD)

5-11-97
adapted

Resources for Pentecost Sunday and Season

A. Calls to Worship

1. LEADER: We have come to celebrate the birthday of the church.
   PEOPLE: We have come to celebrate the gift of the Holy Spirit.
   LEADER: We have come to celebrate Pentecost and to open ourselves to God's Spirit that it might fill us.
   UNISON: O God, help us to put our selfish desires aside and direct our thoughts to you, that your power might fill this church and our lives fully, just as it has filled churches and people throughout the ages. Teach us to be *your* church and *your* people. Amen.
          (PM)

45

2. LEADER: The Spirit blows life through us all.
   PEOPLE: We gather in the renewing life the Spirit gives to us.
   LEADER: Let us then worship with great joy, and celebrate the new life among us.
   PEOPLE: We bring praise and song, joy and laughter before God! Let the world hear our praises! (SEG)

3. *(Quotes phrases from Acts 2:2–3, 17–18 and Isaiah 43:1, RSV)*
   LEADER: Come, believers and faithful ones, sing your alleluias to God!
   PEOPLE: Praise God, who invades us with the rush of a mighty wind and fills us with fire.
   LEADER: Praise God, who out of love for us sent Jesus Christ to live among us.
   PEOPLE: Praise God, whose spirit is poured out upon all flesh so our sons and daughters might prophesy.
   LEADER: God reaches into our lives and claims us, calling us honored and loved.
   PEOPLE: We are God's people: We are redeemed; for God has called us by name.
   UNISON: Come, Holy Spirit, and find us in our wilderness. Lead us forth into the wonders of your love. (JCW)

4. *(Paraphrases parts of the United Church of Christ Statement of Faith)*
   LEADER: The Spirit of God moves among us, binding us in covenant with faithful people of every time and place.
   PEOPLE: The Spirit moves within us, empowering us to proclaim the gospel to all people.
   LEADER: The Spirit moves through us, making us channels of God's love.
   ALL: As we gather to worship, we open ourselves to the Spirit of the living God made known to us in Jesus Christ. Amen. (RCD)

5. LEADER: God's Spirit gives us good and varied gifts.
   LEFT: Praise be to God for the gift of loving one another.
   RIGHT: Praise be to God for the ability to serve one another.
   LEADER: Our lives are enriched by these gifts from God.
   UNISON: Praise be to God that we are bound together as one by the Spirit which gives us these gifts. (PM)

B. Collect for Pentecost

(Paraphrases A.N. Whitehead's description of God's nature as "tender care that nothing be lost," in Process and Reality *[New York: Macmillan Co., 1929], p. 525)*
Gracious God, Living, Eternal Spirit, we thank you that you seek us in tender loving care, lest any be lost. Help us, in the same way, to reach out toward those who may feel alienated or excluded from the Christian community. Send your Spirit upon us, that when we speak the word of your love, people may hear and

understand in their own language as on that Pentecost day so long ago; for we
pray in the name of Jesus Christ. Amen. (RCD)

C. *Benediction for Pentecost*

Let us go now as Spirited people, powerful as the wind in doing God's will,
energetic as fire in extending the love of Christ. Be builders of understanding and
makers of peace. Amen. (GER)

D. *Pastoral Prayer for Pentecost Sunday*

(*Alludes to 1 Corinthians 12:4–13 and John 10:16; 17:11;* RSV; *paraphrases Romans 12:15,* RSV)

Come, Holy Spirit, come:
Enter our lives.
Free us from all fear.
Give us strength to carry on.
Give us hope and joy sufficient for each day.
Come, Holy Spirit, come:
Give us power to be the church.
Impart your many gifts to our members,
    that we may be the body of Christ's presence in the world.
Free us from all fear, and renew our life together.
Come, Holy Spirit, come.
Bind us close together.
May we rejoice with one another's joys and weep with one another's sorrows.
Bind us together,
    not only with the sheep of this fold,
    but all of Christ's people
    around this city and world.
Forgive the pride, prejudice, and self-righteousness which separate us from one
    another.
Come, Holy Spirit, come:
That all may be one in Christ,
    source of all true unity,
    who is with us today and always,
    even to the end of time. Amen. (RCD)

Lectionary-based Resources
for Sundays After Pentecost

A. Calls to Worship

1. (*Ninth Sunday After Pentecost, Year A; paraphrases Romans 8:18–24,* RSV)
   LEADER: Surely the sufferings of this present time are not worth comparing with the glory that is to be revealed to us.
   PEOPLE: All creation waits with eager longing for the revealing of the children of God.
   LEADER: We groan inwardly as we wait;
   PEOPLE: And as we wait we hope for what we do not see.
   UNISON: As we wait and hope, let us worship together. (RDS)

2. (*Eleventh Sunday After Pentecost, Year C; alludes to Romans 8:20; 12:1–12 and Colossians 3:9–10;* RSV)
   LEADER: We give praise and thanks to God,
   PEOPLE: Who has delivered us from futility and from darkened understanding.
   LEADER: We do not live in alienation from God;
   PEOPLE: We are not callous;
   LEADER: For we seek to put off our old nature and be renewed in our minds,
   PEOPLE: Putting on the new nature, created after the likeness of God,
   LEADER: And revealed to us in Jesus Christ. (RDS)

3. (*Thirteenth Sunday After Pentecost, Year B; paraphrases Psalm 1:1–3; Jeremiah 17:7–8; and Proverbs 9:10;* RSV)
   LEADER: The beginning of wisdom is to give reverence to God.
   PEOPLE: God grant us wisdom to worship and live with reverence.
   LEADER: The wise delight to meditate on God's will and way.
   PEOPLE: They are like a tree, planted by streams of water, that yields fruit in season; its leaf does not wither.
   UNISON: We come to worship God with reverence, hoping to send down the roots of righteousness. Glory be to God, to Jesus Christ, and to the Holy Spirit, now and forever. Amen. (RCD)

4. (*Twentieth Sunday After Pentecost, Year C; paraphrases Habakkuk 1:2; 2:3;* RSV)
   LEADER: O God, how long shall I cry for help and you will not hear?
   PEOPLE: Or cry to you, "Violence!" and you will not see?
   LEADER: Yet the vision awaits its time;
   PEOPLE: It hastens to the end—it will not be.
   LEADER: Let us wait for the help of the Holy One. (MSG)

B. Unison Prayers

1. (*Second Sunday After Pentecost, Year B; paraphrases 2 Corinthians 4:6, 8,* RSV)   God, since you are always present to us, enfolding us in your love, we may sometimes be perplexed, but we never despair. We thank you that you have come to us in Jesus the Christ, healing and liberating, showing us who you are. Your light, shining in the face of Christ, is reflected in our hearts. As we see you in Jesus, may others see Christ in us, to the glory of your name. Amen.

(RCD)

2. (*Fifth Sunday After Pentecost, Year B; alludes to Mark 4:35–41,* RSV)   God of creation's beauty and power, Creator of all things in the farthest reaches of time and space, we praise you. Jesus Christ, who had power on earth to calm the seas, the winds, and the human spirit, we worship you. Holy Spirit, source of new creation in our souls, we open ourselves to you. May our amazement at your creative power move us to live on this earth as your true children. Amen.

(RCD)

3. (*Fifth Sunday After Pentecost, Year B; based on Job 38:1–11, 16–18 and Mark 4:35–41,* RSV)   Your grace is near, O God, for you are the God of the storm. You wait in silence for us until we are open to you. Tune us to hear your voice, to face your silence without fear. Speak and bring to us our Savior, Jesus Christ, the giver of your peace. In the name of this one whom we know as the world's Savior, we pray. Amen.

(JCW)

4. (*Seventh Sunday After Pentecost, Year B; paraphrases 2 Corinthians 12:9 and Psalm 51:17,* RSV)   Vulnerable God, whose strength is made perfect in our weakness, we thank you that you receive us as we are. We thank you that you desire our love and gratitude more than our perfection and that the sacrifice you accept is a humble spirit. Help us to trust always in your grace which reaches out to us in Jesus Christ as we gather at his table. Amen.

(RCD)

5. (*Eighth Sunday After Pentecost, Year B; alludes to Mark 6:7–13,* RSV)   Gracious God, we thank you for Jesus Christ, who in compassion for the helpless and harassed crowds, sent out his disciples with words of hope and deeds of love. We look around us today and see the same depths of human need; we know that you send us out with good news now. We humbly and joyfully accept your mission, trusting in Jesus Christ to give us courage and strength. Amen.

(RCD)

6. (*Ninth Sunday After Pentecost, Year A; alludes to Romans 8:18–24,* RSV) Wonderful, amazing God, we gather as those who have caught a glimpse of the glory and the goodness you intend for your creation. The vision you give us makes us ever restless in this world, as we yearn for your fuller revelation in time and history.

Free us, and our world, from all bondage to sin and futility; make us your true daughters and sons, through the creative power of your Holy Spirit, at work within us. Amen.

(RCD)

7. (*Ninth Sunday After Pentecost, Year C; alludes to Luke 10:38–42,* RSV)
God of stillness, God of action, help us to find a proper balance to our lives. Teach us to find the time and space for prayer and learning, like Mary, who studied at the feet of Jesus. May we do our share of common serving, like Martha, who offered her skill in the kitchen. In work and in prayer, may we be worthy disciples of Jesus, the Word of your love. Amen.   (RCD)

8. (*Tenth Sunday After Pentecost, Year C; alludes to Luke 11:1–10,* RSV)   We thank you, gracious God, that you hear us when we pray to you. Make us bold to trust you; make us patient to wait on you. You open wide the door to your heart when we knock; help us to respond by opening to you; through the grace of Jesus Christ. Amen.   (RCD)

9. (*Eleventh Sunday After Pentecost, Year B; alludes to Judges 16:13–17, Ephesians 4:17–24,* RSV)   Amazing God, your Spirit gave strength to Samson and healing power to Jesus when they opened themselves to you. You place the energies of life within us; but without your help, our energies become dissipated, distorted, disordered. Help us to stay close to you; grant us healing and peace; through the power of your Spirit. Amen.   (RCD)

10. (*Twelfth or Thirteenth Sunday After Pentecost, Year C; paraphrases Hebrews 12:1–3,* RSV)   Glorious God, we thank you for the cloud of witnesses, the multitude of the faithful of all ages, who surround us. Considering their example, and looking to Jesus, may we run the race of life faithfully. Encourage us, that we may not grow weary or fainthearted. Help us to accept your gentle discipline, through the grace of Jesus Christ. Amen.   (RCD)

11. (*Sixteenth Sunday After Pentecost, Year C; alludes to Proverbs 9:1–12,* RSV)
God of Wisdom, God of Light, Holy One, help us to rejoice in the truth. Grant that we may experience the meaning of your reign among men and women on this earth, through the grace of Jesus Christ. Amen.   (RCD)

12. (*Eighteenth Sunday After Pentecost, Year C; alludes to Luke 16:10–13,* RSV)
God, keep us faithful in little things. When the task is so small that no one will notice our work, may we still do your bidding. When a smile, a touch, a word could bring sunshine to someone's life, shine through us. Help us to be worthy of your trust in us; through the grace of Jesus Christ. Amen.   (RCD)

C. Prayers of Confession

1. (*Ninth Sunday After Pentecost, Year C; based on Luke 10:38–42,* RSV)
Everflowing God, we gather here needing your love now. We have let the dividing walls of ignorance, war, and greed come between us and our sisters and brothers. Like Martha, we have often only concentrated on our own tasks, and then complained when we see others serve you differently. Like Mary, we truly seek to hear your call to us, but find ourselves limited by the expectations our family and friends, and even our churches have for us. Free us, God, so we might arise, reach out and touch the world with your hope and grace. Amen.
(SEG)

2. (*Seventeenth Sunday After Pentecost, Year C, Common Lectionary; based on Luke 14:7–14, RSV; alludes to Hebrews 3:7–19, RSV*)   When we put off until tomorrow our response to your call, forgive us, O God. When our good intentions are not followed by good actions, have patience with us, O God. When we harden our hearts, making all kinds of excuses why we should not serve you, O God, have mercy. Today when we hear your voice, may we rise up to hear and obey, through the grace of Jesus Christ. Amen.   (RCD)

3. (*Seventeenth Sunday After Pentecost, Year B; alludes to James 2:14–18, RSV*) Gracious God, we acknowledge once again that we fall short of our high calling as your people. If we have wished someone well, while withholding help and support we should have given, forgive us, O God. If we have loudly proclaimed our faith, but then refused to follow Christ, forgive us, O God. Through the power of your Spirit, make us persons of courage, compassion, and integrity; through the grace of Jesus Christ. Amen.   (RCD)

4. (*Nineteenth Sunday After Pentecost, Year B; alludes to Mark 9:42–50, RSV*) Compassionate and merciful God, we confess that we sometimes ignore our responsibilities to you and to humanity. If ever we trample on the rights of others while asserting our own right: God, forgive. If ever we sit by on the sidelines, doing nothing, but criticizing those who do: God, forgive. If ever, by our example and deed, we hurt little ones or cause them to do wrong: God, forgive. Grant, O God, that our lives might be flavored with the Spirit of Jesus Christ, as salt flavors food. Amen.   (RCD)

5. (*Twentieth Sunday After Pentecost, Year A; based on Matthew 21:33–43, RSV*)   Forgive us, O God, that like the vineyard workers we are jealous of your grace. We forget that the good things of our lives are gifts from you rather than rewards we have earned. We seek forgiveness for ourselves but deny forgiveness for others. Forgive us and through your Spirit help us to live in a spirit of gratitude and sharing. Amen.   (RCD)

6. (*Twenty-first Sunday After Pentecost, Year C; alludes to Luke 17:11–19, RSV*) Forgive us, O God, if we have taken the gifts of life for granted, without giving thanks, without sharing. Forgive us, Holy One, if we have refused to hear your voice within our hearts or through the prophets of our day. Help us to put our lives in order, so that we will be worthy to share in the bounty of your realm; through Jesus Christ. Amen.   (RCD)

D. Collect Before the Scriptures

(*Fourteenth Sunday After Pentecost, Year C*)   Prepare us, O God, to hear your word through the scriptures of this day. Confront us with your claims on our lives. Clarify the choices we must make if our lives are to have meaning and purpose. Help us to respond to the One who came as the bread of life so we may know life at its fullest and best. Amen.   (LB)

Resources for Special Sundays After Pentecost

A. *Labor Sunday*

(Alludes to Matthew 11:28, RSV)

LEADER: Come, all who labor and are weighed down with responsibility, uncertainty, and worry.

PEOPLE: We come, because the load we carry is heavier than we can bear alone.

LEADER: Come, all you who seek to relate work and worship, leisure and service, into a meaningful whole.

PEOPLE: We gather for spiritual renewal and practical challenge, for help in making choices and carrying out our commitments.

LEADER: Come, sinner and saint, with your hatreds and loves, your failures and successes, your sorrows and joys.

PEOPLE: We respond to the Spirit's leading and open ourselves to receive God's gracious gifts. (LB)

B. *Native American Sunday*

1. A Responsive Call

LEADER: Eternally Present God, God of all creation, we aspire to be like those who fully felt the movement of the earth as wondrous and treated it as a gift from you.

PEOPLE: Our ways of speed and of progress and development are not always the route to true wisdom which embraces all of life, the quiet forest and the windswept plains and prairies.

LEADER: It is with respect that we remember the many tribes and countless Native Americans that inhabited this continent.

PEOPLE: Yet it is also with a sense of shame and of accountability that we seek to right that which was taken unethically, immorally, and illegally.

LEADER: In the name of justice and of love for our neighbor, may we seek the one true Spirit at work in different ways with different peoples.

PEOPLE: Let us embrace with friendship all of God's creation and listen and learn from the variety of ways that God chooses to touch and embrace us. Amen. (JH)

2. Collect   *(The phrase "O Star-abiding One" is from "Dakota Hymn," ed. Philip Frazier, The Dakota Indian Hymnal.)*

O Star-abiding One, Eternal Spirit, your eye beholds with love all people you have made. Fill us with your Spirit of love that we may share the burdens of humanity, as a sign of bearing the cross of Christ. Hear our prayers for the native peoples of this land, that they may find the justice and dignity due all your children. Through Jesus Christ we pray. Amen. (RCD)

3. Prayer of Confession

Today, O God, we pray for ourselves and our nation, as we remember injustices suffered by the native peoples of our land. There is blood on our hands, even today. Look on us with compassion, Great Spirit, and help us to restore what is lost, renewing our Mother the Earth and realizing justice for all. In the name of Jesus we pray. Amen. (RCD)

C. Worldwide Communion Sunday

1. Responsive Call to Worship (*Alludes to Romans 8:38*, RSV)

LEADER: Throughout God's world this day Christian churches are celebrating the Eucharist as one family dining together in one room under one roof.

PEOPLE: Our sisters and brothers in Africa, Europe, Central America, Asia and in all lands and countries join us in lifting the bread of life and the cup of salvation.

LEADER: Neither powers nor principalities shall stop us nor deter our purpose, our sense of mission, or our challenge to go forth as disciples into every town, village, and crossroad proclaiming the love of Christ for all creation.

PEOPLE: In Christ's love there is no East, no West, no North, no South, but only one Spirit of hope, love, and peace for all.

LEADER: Let us praise Christ! May this holy meal empower each of us to be agents of hope and peace in a time of uncertainty and strife.

PEOPLE: The bread and wine are not for us alone, but are symbols of a universal message that surpasses the might of missiles and the walls of oppression.

LEADER: May Christ bless the worldwide communion of the church this day!

PEOPLE: Praise be to Christ our Creator, Redeemer, and Savior! Amen.

(JH)

2. Collect (*Paraphrases James 3:14, 18*, RSV)

As we gather at your table from all over the world, O God, we pray that all those who come to you in the name of Christ might be one in Spirit. Knead us together in one loaf. Free us from jealousy and selfish ambition; unite us in mission and service to those in need everywhere. May we sow righteousness and harvest peace, through the grace of Jesus Christ. Amen. (RCD)

D. Litany for the Halloween Season

LEADER: We can be overcome by terror. With terrible things happening all around us, we can feel overwhelmed by the evil in the world.

PEOPLE: When we stop and think, we wish that the Halloween spooks were the worst thing we had to face.

LEADER: But the fearsome masks and the outrageous costumes are not as threatening as the real things that human beings do to one another.
PEOPLE: Cruelty against strangers and children, acts of terrorism against innocent people, and crimes ever more horrifying dominate our news.
LEADER: Yet, in the midst of all the evil in the world, we profess a belief in God.
PEOPLE: We believe in God who is good, and in love which overcomes all.
LEADER: For even in the midst of demonic forces, loving people are at work.
PEOPLE: Justice is carried out. Healing takes place. People love and care for their neighbors and for victims of crimes in many places.
LEADER: Terror and cruelty are not the final words.
PEOPLE: The love of God overcomes all things. (SRH)

E. Reformation Sunday

1. Unison Prayer

Living God, we pray this day that the church universal may heed the gospel call to be a people understanding of others, patient toward those with whom we differ, and loving toward those who are outwardly and inwardly hostile to us and to others.

May we celebrate Reformation Sunday as a re-forming of those truths which are the building blocks not of dissent, but of reconciliation and peace.

May the ministry of our family of faith and of the universal family be enlivened by the image of Jesus Christ, the life of the church and the world! Amen and Amen. (JH)

2. Opening Prayer

O God, our Creator and Sustainer and Renewer, we come before you with humble appreciation that your power is expressed toward us in a mighty love.

We are grateful for this opportunity to worship, for the courage and insights of our forebears who cared enough to speak up and speak out for what they believed to be the best ways to return your love, to act upon it. We pray for the strength in ourselves to protest when that is called for and to keep silence when that, too, serves your will.

We cherish the rich heritage of our church. We ask that you alert us to the contemporary meanings of our history and traditions. We seek not to live in the past but by your grace to let the best of the past live through us.

Finally, God, as we enter this time of worship, we open ourselves to your discipline and guidance. We who tend to get out of shape spiritually call upon you to *re*form us into your image, into sturdy and energetic children who are decisively your own.

In Spirit and in truth, be present among us, for we gather and pray in Christ's good name. Amen. (GER)

F. All Saints or Memorial Sunday

1. Call to Awareness

WOMEN/GIRLS: We gather this morning to celebrate the lives of persons we name as saints.

MEN/BOYS: Some of them are living, others have completed their physical lives here on earth.

WOMEN/GIRLS: Some have touched us personally, others have touched and called into question the institutions and structures of our society.

MEN/BOYS: But *all* have shaken our being—all have been examples of lives of wholeness, working for justice.

ALL: We celebrate these persons and their lives in all aspects of God's creation! (WUMC)

2. Collect

Timeless God, we thank you for all those before us who have kept the faith to the end. We thank you for brave souls of deathless fame, and also for those whose names are remembered only by you. Give us wisdom to understand your will, and courage to live as your people in this day; through the grace of Jesus Christ. Amen. (RCD)

3. The Corporate Confession

LEADER: God, you send us saints . . .

PEOPLE: And we imprison them, or nail them on crosses. Have mercy.

LEADER: God, you send us saints . . .

PEOPLE: And we persuade ourselves they are fools, or meddlers or incompetents. Have mercy.

LEADER: God, you send us saints . . .

PEOPLE: And we hate them for reminding us that our comfort requires the poverty of others. Have mercy.

LEADER: God, you send us saints . . .

PEOPLE: And we ignore them. Have mercy.
(Some moments of reflective silence)

Words of Assurance (*Unison*)

God's Word to us is a word of forgiveness, a word of assurance, a word of grace. We are loved and accepted because we are we and God is God and nothing can finally separate us from our Creator, our Parent, our Sustainer. Amen.

(WUMC)

4. (*Paraphrases Revelation 14:13; 1 Thessalonians 4:13–14; 1 Corinthians 15:35, 37, 43, 53; John 14:2, 26–27; 11:25–26; and Wisdom of Solomon 2:3;* RSV)

LEADER: Blessed are the dead who die in Christ from henceforth,

PEOPLE: That they may rest from their labors, for their works shall follow them.

LEADER: Do not be ignorant, friends, concerning those who fall asleep.

PEOPLE: That you sorrow not as those who have no hope;

LEADER: For if we believe that Jesus died and rose again,

PEOPLE: Even so those who have fallen asleep in Jesus will God receive.

LEADER: But someone will say, "How are the dead raised?" and "In what manner of body do they come?"

PEOPLE: That which we sow is not the body that shall be, but a bare grain.

LEADER: But God gives it a body even as it pleases God, and to each seed a body of its own.

PEOPLE: It is sown in dishonor, it is raised in glory. It is sown a natural body, it is raised a spiritual body.

LEADER: For this corruptible must put on incorruption, and this mortal must put on immortality;

PEOPLE: For if the earthly house of our tabernacle be dissolved, we have a building from God, a house not made with hands, eternal in the heavens.

LEADER: Jesus said, "In God's house are many rooms . . . for I go to prepare a place for you."

PEOPLE: "I will not leave you desolate, I will come to you."

LEADER: "The Comforter, the Holy Spirit, shall teach you all things, and bring to you remembrance of all that I have said to you."

PEOPLE: "Peace I leave with you. My peace I give to you. Do not let your hearts be troubled, neither let them be afraid."

LEADER: "For I am the resurrection and the life. Those who believe in me, though they be dead, shall yet be alive."

PEOPLE: "And whoever believes in me shall never die."

LEADER: For God created all people to be immortal, and made us in the divine eternal image.

PEOPLE: The souls of the righteous are in the hand of God, and there no evil can touch them.

LEADER: They are in peace and their hope is full of immortality.

PEOPLE: For God has tested them, and found them worthy. Amen.

(RLA)

G. Thanksgiving

1. Call to Worship   (Based on Psalm 107, RSV)

LEADER: O give thanks to God for all the goodness we are shown! God's steadfast love endures forever!

PEOPLE: We come from the east and the west, the north and the south, to give God thanks and praise!

LEADER: We once were a wandering people, hungry and thirsty in a desert land.

PEOPLE: We cried to God to deliver us, and we were led to a new land rich in promise and harvest.

UNISON: We give thanks for God's steadfast love! God quenches the thirsty, fills the hungry, and leads us from the desert land to a harvest home. (JCW)

2. Unison Prayer of Invocation

God of the harvest, from seed and sun you have blessed us with a harvest to help feed the world. For this we give you our highest thanks. You also offer us seed and sun for the times of famine in our lives. In the times we know the famine of silence and grief, cause us to remember you as the God of harvest. For with you, the faith we offer serves as seed for the harvest of your life-giving food. In Christ's name. Amen. (JCW)

3. Prayer

Dear God, it is hard for us to thank you with a head full of worries and a heart full of troubles. Sometimes we have to complain to you before we feel free to love you. O God, our lives can be so difficult. Some of our days have been filled with heartache, loss, confusion, sickness, and death. Sometimes, God, you have seemed far off and impossible to understand. God, we wish we could understand why life must be so painful.

We know that the hurt has stretched and deepened us. And we know that you suffer alongside and with us. Help us to know the secret of resurrection; show us how to move on from suffering to rebirth. Go with us now. Go with us now as we move on. Dear God, go with us. Amen. (HAS)

Resources Appropriate for All Seasons

Calls to Worship

A. Responsive Calls to Worship

1. (*Alludes to Luke 3:16,* RSV)
   LEADER: In the darkness and emptiness of much we call life, the Spirit moves among us, calling us into new being.
   PEOPLE: We are here to seek light amid the shadows, fulfillment out of hollowness and despair.
   LEADER: From separation and bitterness, apathy and hatred, God, in Christ, calls us to steadfast love and reconciliation.
   PEOPLE: We have come to find healing and peace, to experience forgiveness, acceptance, and purpose.
   LEADER: In the midst of the ordinary, God has come to us. In our everyday worlds, God continues to visit and redeem.
   PEOPLE: Come, Holy Spirit, to baptize us with fire. We await your word and the power of your benediction. (LB)

2. (*Paraphrases Revelation 7:9, 12; 4:8; 5:12; Isaiah 6:3;* RSV; *and the Sanctus*)
   LEADER: Let us gather with the faithful from every nation, race, people, and language, in worshiping the God made known to us in Jesus Christ.
   PEOPLE: To God, the Ruler of the universe, and to Jesus, the Lamb, be blessing and honor, glory and might forever and ever.
   LEADER: Let us gather in God's presence, singing songs of praise and joy with the people of God in every place and time.
   PEOPLE: Holy, holy, holy, great God of Hosts! The whole earth is full of your glory. Glory be to you, O God most high. Amen. (RCD)

3. (*Paraphrases Psalm 122:1,* RSV)
   LEADER: I was glad when they said to me, let us go to the house of the Living God.
   PEOPLE: This is the day when we rejoice in God's act of creation.
   LEADER: This is our sabbath, when we rejoice in the resurrection of Jesus the Christ.
   PEOPLE: We give thanks that once more, God has brought us together, that we might refresh one another.
   ALL: Peace to all who enter here, peace this day and every day, in the name of Jesus Christ. Amen. (RCD)

4. LEADER: When we stumble and our faith falters, God's faithfulness bears us along.
   LEFT SIDE: When our spirits soar and our faith grows strong, God's faithfulness lifts us to new heights of devotion.
   RIGHT SIDE: When our daily duties distract, and our visions grow fuzzy, God's faithfulness pierces the fog to beckon us.
   UNISON: God's faithfulness endures forever! We lift our hearts in praise to the One who is our God this day and forever more!

   (PM)

5. LEADER: The God of New Beginnings has called us to this place.
   PEOPLE: We come celebrating the new life that is ours as God's faithful people.
   LEADER: Let your joy ring through the universe, and let your vision see to the depths of every soul.
   PEOPLE: We will be shouters of joy and seekers of God's light wherever we go. Praise God for this day! (SEG)

6. LEADER: God is very near to us.
   PEOPLE: We come together to praise God who lives and dwells among us.
   LEADER: Bring your songs and your praises and let the Spirit of God be heard in this place!
   PEOPLE: We praise God with song and voice: with dance and laughter, and we greet one another with love.
   ALL: Praise be to God! Alleluia! Amen. (SEG)

7. (*Quotes a phrase from the hymn "Just As I Am" by Charlotte Elliott*)
   LEADER: We gather today, seeking the peace Christ gives.
   PEOPLE: We gather, in spite of many a conflict, many a doubt, within our souls.
   LEADER: We gather, longing for the breath of God's Spirit to give us courage and renewal.
   ALL: Come, Christ Jesus, be our guest. Bless us through the power of your Spirit, and give us the courage to live as your disciples day by day. Amen. (RCD)

8. (*Based on Psalms 46 and 131,* JB, NEB, RSV)
   LEADER: God calls us in the midst of our lives:
   PEOPLE: "Pause a while and know that I am God."
   LEADER: God calls us from our lofty ambitions, our haughtiness, from our occupations with marvels and matters beyond our scope:
   PEOPLE: "Let be and learn that I am God."
   LEADER: Come, behold the astounding things God has done in the world.
   PEOPLE: God is our shelter, our strength, ever ready to help in time of trouble.
   LEADER: People of God, hope in our God.
   PEOPLE: Enough for us to calm and quiet our souls like a child quieted at its mother's breast.

LEADER: God is with us, now and forevermore!

PEOPLE: Amen. (LGS)

9. (*Quotes the song "Spirit of the Living God" by Daniel Iverson; alludes to Luke 22:26–27, RSV*)

LEADER: Spirit of the Living God, fall afresh on us. As we gather in this place, allow your spirit to fill our very being.

PEOPLE: As we worship today, we remember our brothers and sisters who are worshiping elsewhere throughout the world. Inspire each of us to work more faithfully for justice and dignity of life everywhere.

LEADER: Raise our vision above the barriers of color, culture, and creed that separate us. Give us wisdom as we deal with one another; help us to recognize and to respect different ways, rather than to judge.

PEOPLE: In the spirit of Jesus who came not to be served but to serve, we now must walk in the world, we now must reach out our hands with help and open our hearts in love. Awake in us the desire to seek your way of serving you in the world.

LEADER: Come, people of God, rejoice!

PEOPLE: Come, let us worship together. (NRM)

10. LEADER: God has been acting in our lives and in the world around us this past week.

PEOPLE: We have come for this hour of worship to make ourselves more aware of God and to give thanks for God's presence with us.

LEADER: God is here even now, ready to strengthen us and to urge us to greater faithfulness.

UNISON: Fill us with your goodness, O God. Draw us into the orbit of your activity in the world that we might fulfill the purpose for which you created us. Amen. (PM)

11. LEADER: And God created the heavens and the earth.

PEOPLE: And gave them to us to use and enjoy.

LEADER: And God breathed life into each of us, and set us upon the earth.

PEOPLE: And God sent Jesus Christ to save us from the pull of death.

LEADER: Everything that fills our souls with gladness and light is a gift from the loving Creator.

PEOPLE: We have been entrusted with unfathomable riches. For all this our God is to be praised. Let us worship God together! (RDS)

12. LEADER: From the ends of the earth we are gathered together;

PEOPLE: The poor, and the rich, the joyful, the sorrowful, the honored, and the despised—

LEADER: All are gathered in one community,

PEOPLE: Reflecting the love and life of God.

ALL: We have come from many worlds. Let us worship God as one! (MSG)

13. LEADER: Gracious and loving Creator, we come today in summery joy;

PEOPLE: We come to celebrate your love in our midst;
LEADER: We come here secure and assured—
PEOPLE: Of your forgiveness and truth,
LEADER: Your salvation and joy,
PEOPLE: Your sustaining love and your alluring will.
LEADER: Yet in this hour we know, too, and confess our weakness—
PEOPLE: Our faltering faith and our rancorous lives.
LEADER: Lead us, great God, in faith, through the hours and days ahead,
PEOPLE: To glorify you and to serve one another.   (RDS)

14. LEADER: Let us praise God.
PEOPLE: Let us praise the One who has filled the earth with blessings.
LEADER: Let us sing to the Creator who has filled our lives with joy.
PEOPLE: Sorrows befall us;
LEADER: Troubles besiege us;
PEOPLE: The prophets of God disturb us,
LEADER: Yet we live supported by God's love. Amen.   (MSG)

15. LEADER: Listen, for the voice of God comes near!
PEOPLE: Listen, for God's voice is not obtrusive.
LEADER: We come to worship the God who became one of us,
PEOPLE: Who calls us by name,
LEADER: Who is Love Incarnate,
PEOPLE: Who is!
LEADER: Let us gather together in joy and hope—
PEOPLE: Let us worship the God of Love!   (RDS)

16. LEADER: Great Spirit, you have turned your face earthward and opened your heart to your children,
PEOPLE: And so, O God, do we turn to you now.
LEADER: We turn to you for purpose and correction,
PEOPLE: For joy and peace,
LEADER: For a way out of hopeless situations,
PEOPLE: For justice,
LEADER: For forgiveness,
PEOPLE: For love.
LEADER: We turn to you, O God, for all these things offered through Jesus the Christ, the maker of redemption and the bringer of hope.
PEOPLE: Amen.   (RDS)

17. (Based on Psalm 48, TEV)
LEADER: God is great, and highly to be praised, in the holy city, on God's sacred hill.
PEOPLE: Zion, the mountain of God, is high and beautiful: It brings joy to all the earth.
LEADER: Inside your temple, O God, we consider your constant love!
PEOPLE: You are praised by people everywhere, and your fame extends over all the earth.

LEADER: You rule with justice; let the people of Zion be glad!
PEOPLE: Guide us for all time to come, O God; we are yours forever. Amen. (RCD)

18. LEADER: People of God, look about creation and see the faces of those we know and love—neighbors and friends, brothers and sisters—a communion of kindred hearts.

PEOPLE: People of God, look about and see the faces of those we hardly know—strangers, sojourners, forgotten friends, the ones who need an outstretched hand, for signs of healing, hope and love.

LEADER: People of God, look about and see all the images of God assembled here today. In me, in you, in each of us everywhere, God's Spirit shines for all to see!

PEOPLE: : People of God, come, let us worship together. (AAW)

19. (*Paraphrases Psalm 57:7–10, RSV*)
LEADER: Our hearts are steadfast, O God, our hearts are steadfast!
PEOPLE: We will sing and make melody!
LEADER: Awake, awake my soul! Awake, O harp and lyre!
PEOPLE: We will awake the dawn!
LEADER: We will give thanks to thee, O God, among the peoples;
PEOPLE: We will sing praises to thee among the nations.
LEADER: For thy steadfast love is great to the heavens,
PEOPLE: Thy faithfulness is great to the clouds. (RDS)

20. LEADER: In this land of freedom and beauty, let us give thanks to God.
PEOPLE: Let us praise the Holy One who created the blue lakes and grassy prairies, the vast desert lands, and the breathtaking mountains of our homeland.
LEADER: Let us unite in worship of the Creator who formed all lands and all people,
PEOPLE: And who declared, without hesitation, "It is good."
LEADER: Come, let us worship God. (MSG)

21. (*Paraphrases Isaiah 43:19, RSV*)
LEADER: Behold, God is doing a new thing.
PEOPLE: Here. Now. In the midst of our routines.
LEADER: The Holy One who created heaven and earth forms us afresh today.
PEOPLE: Let our spirits rise to greet our Maker.
ALL: Amen! (MSG)

22. (*Paraphrases Psalm 92:1–4, RSV*)
LEADER: It is good to give thanks to you, O God,
PEOPLE: To declare your steadfast love in the morning;
LEADER: For you have made us glad by your work;
PEOPLE: At the works of your hands, we sing for joy. (MSG)

23. LEADER: We give praise and thanks to our God,

PEOPLE: Who delivers us from futility and from darkened understanding.
LEADER: Who is our hope in hard times—
PEOPLE: Our mighty and everlasting hope,
LEADER: Who is our joy to please,
PEOPLE: And our salvation every day.
LEADER: Come, let us worship our God.   (RDS)

24. (*Based on Psalm 29*, RSV)
LEADER: Ascribe to God glory and strength! Ascribe to God's name glory and power!
PEOPLE: The voice of God is upon the waters, full of majesty! and might!
LEADER: The voice of God breaks the cedars, and thunders across the forest.
PEOPLE: The voice of God flashes forth flames of fire and shakes the wilderness.
UNISON: May God give us strength, for we are God's people! May God bless us with peace and grant us grace!   (JCW)

25. LEADER: We are called from the ends of the earth.
PEOPLE: We are called from the dead centers of our lives.
LEADER: We are called to praise God.
PEOPLE: We are called to serve the Holy One.
LEADER: God has breathed into us the breath of new life. Let us worship with joy.   (MSG)

26. LEADER: It is God our Maker who sets us free to live,
PEOPLE: Who calls us into a community of freedom and commitment.
LEADER: It is Jesus our Christ who has blazed the trail of new life,
PEOPLE: Who has gone before us to overcome sin and death.
LEADER: It is the Spirit of peace that binds us as one,
PEOPLE: Who flows among us like a healing river.
ALL: Glory be to God the Maker, Christ, and Spirit, in all that we say and do here! Amen.   (RCD)

27. LEADER: Listen to the good news. God is with us, this day and every day.
PEOPLE: Because God is with us, we can face each day with courage. We can find some good in everything, for we are never completely alone.
LEADER: God's goodness sometimes seems to be a trickle, sometimes pulsing spurts, and sometimes a mighty flood. But always God is with us.
UNISON: We worship you, O God, for your goodness. We praise you with our songs. We seek you in our prayers. We offer ourselves to you because you are our God.   (PM)

28. LEADER: As in the days of Jesus the blind received their sight,
PEOPLE: So may we see you, O Gracious Savior.
LEADER: As we receive our sight, as we see you more clearly,
PEOPLE: May we also see our sister and our brother; the hungry and the poor, those who are black, brown, white, yellow; those who live

next door, and those who live half a world away; all of them are neighbor to us when we call you Christ.

UNISON: Open our eyes as we sing, open our hearts as we pray, open our lives as we worship you this day. (BJW)

29. LEADER: This is a new day filled with fresh possibilities.
PEOPLE: We gather to participate in the new things God is doing.
LEADER: Old ways and tired routines are left behind.
PEOPLE: Our God comes to us in unexpected ways and refreshes all who join the adventure.
LEADER: Those who claim sophistication and power may miss the movement of the eternal.
PEOPLE: All who give up their pretenses will find unusual opportunities.
LEADER: Let us together explore the wonders of God.
PEOPLE: Create in us clean hearts, O God, and renew our spirits.
LEADER: Amen. (LB)
PEOPLE: Amen.

30. LEADER: We come to church this morning seeking healing in our lives: healing of physical and mental illness; healing of painful memories; healing of broken relationships.
PEOPLE: Worship is a time when we bring our brokenness to God and ask for a mending of the pieces. Let us pray to God for our healing where we need it most.
LEADER: O God, we pray that upon leaving this place this morning, we may have experienced insight into our need for your love.
UNISON: Bring light to the dark corners of our souls. Amen. (HWW)

31. LEADER: God our Creator, you have given us life, one gift we are not able to create by our own skills.
PEOPLE: That life is a story not yet finished. You have given us the opportunity to fill that life with what you would have us do.
LEADER: Grant us wisdom, O God, to discern between your work and our own. Let our work be yours.
PEOPLE: Help us to be aware of our limitations and capabilities. When we merge our lives with others, we know you will be there.
LEADER: Grant us the understanding to know ourselves in our weakness, for you have given us what we could not give ourselves. Let us pass on what we have received from you.
PEOPLE: Create in us your Spirit that we may choose to learn to minister in your name.
LEADER: O God, we can go far, but no farther, without your guidance. We know you will be our guide through the darkness of life.
UNISON: Take us to you; heal us, strengthen us to touch the lives of others with your changing Spirit. Amen. (HWW)

32. (Paraphrases Psalm 133:1, 3, RSV, TEV, and Psalm 111:1, RSV)
LEADER: Oh, how good and pleasant it is for God's people to live together in oneness.

PEOPLE: It is like the dew on Mount Hermon, falling on the hills of Zion.

LEADER: For there God has promised blessing: life that never ends.

ALL: We will give thanks to God with our whole hearts, in the company of God's people, in the congregation. Praise be to God. Amen.

(RCD)

33. (*Paraphrases Psalm 98:4–9*, TEV)

LEADER: Sing for joy to God, all the earth;

PEOPLE: Worship with songs and shouts of joy!

LEADER: Sing praise to God! Play music on the harps!

PEOPLE: Blow trumpets and horns, and shout for joy to the Holy One of Israel!

LEADER: Roar, sea, and every creature in you;

PEOPLE: Sing, earth, and all who live on you!

LEADER: Clap your hands, you rivers; you hills, sing together before God.

PEOPLE: God comes to rule the earth, and to govern the peoples of the earth with justice and fairness.

(MAN)

34. LEADER: In faith, Abraham and Sarah set out for a new land.

PEOPLE: In faith, we seek to follow God in our lives.

LEADER: In faith, the church continually seeks to understand what tasks God has set before us at the present moment.

PEOPLE: In faith, we gather now to worship, knowing that as we reach out to God, God will make us new. Give us the faith, O God, to go forward and embrace the newness to which you call us.

(PM)

35. (*Paraphrases Isaiah 49:15–16*, RSV)

LEADER: Have you ever felt abandoned by God?

PEOPLE: Yes, oh, yes.

LEADER: But God says, "I will never forget you!"

PEOPLE: How can this be so?

LEADER: God says, "I have written your name on the palms of my hands."

PEOPLE: The God who created us, sustains and re-creates us, remembers and calls us.

LEADER: We come, remembering and worshiping God who cares for us.

(BJW)

6-23-86   Install.

36. (*Alludes to Isaiah 49:1*, RSV)

LEADER: God has created us, called us from our mother's wombs and formed of us a people.

PEOPLE: No longer are we lonely individuals, but part of the whole human race, living and sharing with others.

LEADER: We discover life to be so complex. It is tears; it is smiles; it is joy; it is sorrow.

PEOPLE: It is a gift from God. Laugh, cry, sing, be silent; in whatever way we live, be thankful unto God! Amen!

(BJW)

37. (*Paraphrases Romans 8:39,* RSV)
    LEADER: We come to hear the story of God's faithfulness to past generations.
    PEOPLE: But we are looking to the future, not the past.
    LEADER: Our God is also God of the future, the God who was with our ancestors will be with us as well.
    PEOPLE: Then we can go forward in hope. Whatever else fails, God remains faithful. Nothing can separate us from the love of God! Praise be to God! (PM)

38. (*Paraphrases Psalm 118:24,* RSV)
    LEADER: God calls us this day to a life of joy.
    PEOPLE: With God, joy cracks through the bonds of despair.
    LEADER: With God, joy bursts forth from moments of quiet pleasure.
    PEOPLE: With God, joy gilds the edges of even ordinary days.
    UNISON: This is the day which our God has made; let us rejoice and be glad in it. (PM)

39. (*Quotes Exodus 34:6,* RSV)
    LEADER: God is merciful and gracious, slow to anger, and abounding in steadfast love and faithfulness.
    PEOPLE: We have gathered to hear the story of God and God's people.
    LEADER: It is a story of God's mercy and steadfast love.
    PEOPLE: It is our story, for we are God's people.
    UNISON: Inspire us, our God, to faithfulness, to mercy, to steadfast love. Let us become a people who reflect your image. (PM)

40. (*Alludes to the hymn "Morning Has Broken" by Eleanor Farjeon*)
    LEADER: The morning light has broken through the darkness of the night once again.
    PEOPLE: In such a manner God's light and word breaks into our lives.
    LEADER: God breaks through all the confusion, doubt, and loneliness which absorb us at times. God's light shines on us and reveals all that is within us, and within God's creation.
    PEOPLE: We are promised this continued in-breaking of the Spirit. The Spirit breaks in on us today with the glad news: Today is God's day.
    ALL: In this day we delight in praising the God who loves us. All praises for God's re-creation of this new day. (BJW)

41. (*Alludes to Jeremiah 31:33,* RSV)
    LEADER: In truth and love, God has called us into this house of worship. God has said to us,
    PEOPLE: "You are my people, I am your God."
    LEADER: Not once, but again and again the Word is spoken, and there is rejoicing over all the earth. The words ring out with a glad cry:
    PEOPLE: "You are my people, I am your God. You are my people, close to my heart."

LEADER: Come, O people of God; let us be glad as we sing God's praises; for our Creator and Redeemer has said:

PEOPLE: "You are my people, I am your God. You are my people, close to my heart."

LEADER: With awe and wonder, in the spirit of grace we lift our voices unto the God of creation, who redeems us and keeps us by the power of grace which comes from the God we worship this day.

(BJW)

42. (*Paraphrases 1 John 4:19*, RSV)

LEADER: Out of the fullness of the lives God has given us we have come to worship and to praise.

PEOPLE: With thanks we offer to God the creativity of our minds, the warmth of our hearts, and the joy of our spirits.

LEADER: We love because God has first loved us, freeing us from the power of sin and death.

PEOPLE: With glad hearts let us join together in singing praise to God, Creator, Word, and Holy Spirit. Amen. (RCD)

43. (*Based on Psalm 8:1, 3–5, 9*, RSV)

LEADER: O God, our God, how glorious is your name in all the earth!

PEOPLE: Your glory is sung by all of your creation!

LEADER: When we look to the heavens, the work of your fingers, the moon and the stars, we wonder—

PEOPLE: Who are we that you care for us and for this world?

UNISON: You are the God of life, crowning us with glory and honor to serve you all our days. O God, our God, how glorious is your name in all the earth! (JCW)

44. (*Paraphrases Psalm 30:1, 4, 5, 10–12*, RSV)

LEADER: Sing praises to God, O you saints, and give thanks to God's holy name!

PEOPLE: We exalt you, O God, for you have restored us to life!

LEADER: We may cry through the night, but your joy comes with the morning.

PEOPLE: You hear us, O God, and you are gracious in our distress.

UNISON: You turn our mourning into dancing! Our souls cannot be silent! O God our Savior, we give thanks to you forever! (JCW)

45. (*Paraphrases Psalm 81:1, 5–7, 9, 16*, RSV)

LEADER: Sing aloud to God our strength! Shout for joy to the God of Israel!

PEOPLE: We hear a voice we have not before known. It is God's voice saying, "In distress you called and I delivered you."

LEADER: "I answered you in the secret place of thunder. There shall be no strange god among you, nor shall you bow down to any foreign god."

PEOPLE: "For I am your God! I will feed you with the finest of wheat and with honey from the rock."

UNISON: Sing aloud to God our strength! Shout for joy to our God, the
God of Israel! (JCW)

46. (*Paraphrases Psalm 24:1–2, 9–10*, RSV)
LEADER: The earth and all that is in it belongs to God,
PEOPLE: For God has made the sea its foundation and made it firm upon the
rivers of the deep.
LEADER: So let us rejoice in God and in all creation.
PEOPLE: We shall rejoice in the God of Hosts, the God of Glory!
UNISON: Lift up your heads, O gates! Lift them high, O everlasting doors!
For the God of Glory shall enter and reign over us all!
(JCW)

47. (*Based on Psalm 103*, RSV)
LEADER: With all that is within us, let us bless God,
PEOPLE: Who forgives all our sins, who heals all our diseases,
LEADER: Who lifts us up from rock bottom, who crowns us with steadfast
love and mercy.
ALL: With all that is within us, let us give praise and thanks to God,
who creates, redeems, and sustains us. Amen. (RCD)

B. Opening Sentences or Prayers

1. We will lift our hearts to you, our Maker, like spring flowers to the sun. We
will drink your living water until we are filled with the Spirit. We will reach out
to you and bask in your loving presence. Amen. (HAS)

2. Be with us, our God and our Friend. Come to your people and lift their
troubled hearts. Take our burdens and blindness and free us to come to you.
Amen. (HAS)

3. God, we come to you empty, praying to be filled. Come, fill our lives with
meaning and power through your Spirit. Amen. (HAS)

4. (*Paraphrases Psalm 100:2, 4*, RSV)
LEADER: God, we are seeking you:
PEOPLE: Let yourself be found. *11-17-96*
LEADER: God, we are calling you:
PEOPLE: Listen to our prayers.
ALL: We enter your courts with singing. We walk through your gates
with thanksgiving. Receive your people with gladness! Welcome us
with blessings! (HAS)

C. Opening Statements

1. Yesterday as a child, I entered church as though walking into a treasure chest
of colors and sounds and meaning deep and mysterious; today I enter church

with less awe and wonder but more ease and familiarity as a member of the household; tomorrow the door of a new realm opens and my eyes grow wide as I peek and tiptoe in—I will be a child again.

Yesterday as a child the seeds of faith were sown within me and I believed the improbable and impossible with a cherishable, imperishable trust in a God more than Superman or Wonder Woman; today the seeds have sprouted into plants perhaps spindly or gnawed at by pests like nibbling selfishness or munching worldly values; tomorrow the fruit of God's vineyard will ripen to a sweet taste and my mouth will be wide in a juicy grin of contentment at the Creator's bountiful feast—I will be a child again.

Yesterday we were babes in the faith, today we are growing in it, tomorrow we will mature to belief and become as children again. We gather to worship the God of our yesterdays, todays, and tomorrows. (GER)

2. God calls us together to worship this morning. From our work and play within the world, God gathers us to give thanks for creation's goodness, for the strength to labor, for the wisdom to relax.

From amidst our friends and family God brings us here to participate in a community of faith, Christ's people, a new family.

From everyday conversations, talk, and chatter, God invites us to engage one another in dialogue, to speak in truth from the depths of heart and mind, to pray freely.

Let us heed God's call and rejoice in what God enables. Welcome to worship.

An Opening Prayer   (*For use with the above call*)

O God, in our time of worship, and throughout the hours of our days, remain at the center of our thoughts and actions. When all that we do seems to fly off in scattered bits and pieces as our lives spin on, draw us back to you. Hold us together as individuals and as a community of faith. In our looking outward into time and toward your creation, enable us to focus our hopes and to hit the mark when we aim to do your will. Be for us a home base, a center of gravity, a balance point, a source of loving support through Christ Jesus in whose name we pray. Amen. (GER)

3. We come to this place, God, because somewhere in our lives, faintly or distinctly, we have heard you call to us.

We come—some sleepily, some alert, some tired, some energized—to share in your presence.

We come to say thanks that we are your people. We come to worship, to know better what your call upon us means. (ME)

4. There is a well in this place filled with care, mutual acceptance, strength, and love. Supplied by God, it is kept fresh by the people you see near you now. I have contributed to this source and I have drawn from it; maybe you have too. By the grace of God it never empties. It is the church: the koinonia, the people of God, the communion of believers, brothers and sisters we can touch and love, surrounded by God's presence, here and everywhere. (KFK)

D. Bulletin Statement About the Time Before Worship

The Time of Centering: We use this time to make the transition between "getting here" and "being here." Take these few minutes of quiet time to get in touch with the calm places, the still, deep places in you; the spirit. Relax your body; quiet the inner dialogue of your mind. Focus on feeling, on being. Be receptive to your center—your reservoir of inner peace, strength, love. Be aware of being with others. Feel the spirit of the community. (WUMC)

Invocations

1. God of this new day, we praise you with joy! You take our weary lives and refresh us with your spirit. Our lives so often seem broken and filled with despair. Heal us this day, God, and make us new. Amen. (SEG)

2. We greet you, welcoming God, with our many morning moods. Some of us could not wait to get here; some of us just made it. Some of us know exactly why we've come; others are not sure. Still, something calls us each to you and we come to seek and to worship.

    We remember before you all that has made life good in recent days—the dear, daily love of family and friends, the satisfaction of work well done, the sweetness of a good night's sleep. For any and all things which make us glad to be alive, we rejoice!

    And we remember, also, all people who do not share our rejoicing or who do so even while in peril—the lonely, the sick, those imprisoned or at war. For our sisters and brothers facing any distress, we pray your strength and peace will find and sustain them.

    And, though it is hard for us, we pray for those we dislike and mistrust, hoping that they, too, pray for us. Grant that these prayers may open our eyes and hearts to one another and so make "love" and "peace" more than slogans in the church and the world. Because you love us, because we love you, may this be so! Amen. (ABD)

3. Since, dear God, like a father you daily guard us against evil, and like a mother you constantly bring us gifts of goodness; give us, we pray, your Holy Spirit, that witnessing your goodness, we may always praise your kindness, through the grace of Jesus Christ. (DB)

4. God, your changes touch our lives with mystery and hope. We come to this place today, ready to see your power working through us. Help us to be open to your Word, and to answer your call among us. Through Jesus Christ we pray. Amen. (SEG)

5. God, with great gentleness and care, you call us to be your people and to do your work. Be here with us today, for we come, asking for your support in all that

we do. We need your love, transforming our lives in hope. Be with us, we pray. Amen. (SEG)

6. You who have created us and who sustains us: We come with thanksgiving for these moments when we can ease the pace of our lives and listen for your voice. Create a spirit within us that truly draws us toward you and toward our brothers and sisters: a spirit deep, perceptive, gentle, and bold. Clear our minds, open our hearts, and touch us with your presence and your power. We offer this prayer in the name of Jesus Christ our friend and our Savior. Amen. (CHS)

7. O God, for the sun and the stars, the mountains and the valleys, we your children come to you offering our thanks and seeking your presence. Be among us, opening our hearts to the sway of your power and your peace.

We dedicate this service to you. We trust that you will work through our songs and our sayings so that we will leave this place knowing your hand has touched us. Amen. (CHS)

8. Creator God, most distant space shows traces of your touch. Sculptor God, you give galaxies their form, shape granite mountains, and design butterfly wings. You choreograph the paths of stars and the flight of snow geese. Your divine song is sung by sparrows, mountain streams, and the rushing winds. We human beings wonder at all you create and rejoice to be a part of the living world which you love and sustain. Amen. *7-21-96* (SLB)

9. *(For a special day)* Gracious God, the excitement and joy of this day surrounds us. Laughter comes easily to our lips. How long we have prepared for this hour! Help us remember that it is not our own doing that brings us here, but only your grace and love. Your love has surrounded us from our birth even when we have not seen it. Your love has been present in your word and in the words and acts of others. For this we give you thanks. Teach us to walk gently in your path of love, seeking justice, making peace, cherishing the earth and one another. Enliven our imaginations that we can see through present ills to future newness. Embolden us with your love, that we may live now as if the new had already come. In joy we offer you our praise. Amen. (MAM)

10. We can feel it within ourselves, each of us, our creativity awaiting life. Its voice whispers to us, forming that vision which is so intimately our own, yet asks to be shared. The words that require a page, the forms of color begging a canvas, the motion that needs to be danced, or the pattern of sounds which may breathe only through a flute.

Dear God, help us to recognize these voices in ourselves; challenge us to realize them to life, in beauty; and help us to feel your presence in their whispers. Amen. (LS)

11. God of grace and glory, make your presence known to us as we worship this morning.

Jesus our Christ, may your name be praised from the rising of the sun to the midnight hour; may your name always be honored among us.

Spirit of Holiness, breathe on us all and bind us in Christian love and servant-hood.

O God, Creator, Christ and Holy Spirit, be known to us today. Transform our lives and our community into the image of Jesus Christ, in whose name we pray. Amen. (RCD)

12. God, you have not forsaken us or forgotten us: you are here with us in the blooming of this new day. Help us to wake up to your new day; this day and every day. Alleluia! Amen. (SEG)

13. (*Alludes to Psalm 19:14 and Acts 17:28*, RSV)   O God in whom we live and move and have our being, we have gathered in your presence to sing your praise. Gather up the prayer of each heart into one harmony of worship and service, that we might truly be one body in Christ. Accept the words of our mouths and the thoughts of our hearts, for we are yours in Christ Jesus. Amen. (RCD)

14. Gracious God, we gather this morning in this house of worship which, thanks to your love, is our home away from home. We come to add our human voices to the chorus of praise raised to you by wind and water and all life upon the land! We come as we are—distracted and weary, hopeful and open—knowing that you accept us and are ever mindful of our cares and joys. Still in us now the many voices that clamor for attention, that we might center ourselves upon you. Speak to us, Spirit of Life, in word and melody and quiet, that we may be renewed in our faith and strengthened for your service. This we ask in Christ's name. Amen.

(ABD)

15. God of Love, you have loved us first and continue to love us. We come before you a people longing to love you in return. We hunger for your healing love in our lives, for we long to love ourselves and our neighbors. Come to us this day and fill our longing. In Christ's name, we pray. Amen. (JCW)

Prayers of Confession

A. A Call to Confession

Too often our hearts are cold and without gratitude.
Too often our hands are passive and unwilling to carry out acts of mercy.
Too often our lips are pursed tightly, unwilling to speak words of love.
Too often we are indeed separated and alienated from our better self, separated and alienated from God.
Let us confess our separation and alienation.
Let us join together in the prayer of confession. (RNE)

B. Litanies of Confession

1. LEADER: I was downtown shopping for designer sheets when an old man whispered,

   PEOPLE: I have no bed.

   LEADER: I stood at an appliance store comparing consumer reports on microwave ovens when an African woman wept,

   PEOPLE: I have no food.

   LEADER: I hired a decorator to remodel my kitchen and to add more cupboards when a Cambodian child sobbed,

   PEOPLE: I have no cup.

   LEADER: I dreamed of building a getaway place, a cabin in the woods, a country place. Across the water came the cry,

   PEOPLE: I have no country.

   LEADER: I bought a new big-screen color TV for a loved one's pleasure when a war orphan murmured,

   PEOPLE: I have no loved ones.

   UNISON: May God forgive us when our ears won't hear and our eyes won't see the sounds and sights of suffering around us. Amen.

   (HWW)

2. *(Alludes to Amos 7:7–9, RSV)*

   ALL: We praise the Spirit which unites us as one people. But the plenitude of our gifts disturbs us. We seek to know the truth, but trust only our own truth.

   NORTH: We seek to feed the hungry, but trust only the manna gathered by our own hands.

   SOUTH: We seek to see the plumb line hanging in our midst, but tilt our heads and move our bodies to see the angle that we want.

   ALL: We have failed to celebrate the life gifts of all persons. We have failed, even in this community, to feed and be fed with those gifts. We have failed to work and to wait for justice.   (WUMC)

3. *(Alludes to Ephesians 2:13–16, RSV)*

   LEADER: In Jesus Christ, God broke the barrier of sin and pain which separates us from our neighbor, ourselves, and our God. We seek God's grace so we might move from alienation to new life.

   PEOPLE: So God, grant us new life in you.

   LEADER: When we deny your presence in our busy days—

   PEOPLE: O God, grant us new life in you.

   LEADER: When we feel justified in our anger and resentment toward others—

   PEOPLE: O God, grant us new life in you.

   LEADER: When we judge others before looking at ourselves—

   PEOPLE: O God, grant us new life in you.

   LEADER: When we occupy ourselves in worldly matters and reject your peace and assurance—

PEOPLE: O God, grant us new life in you.

LEADER: When we refuse to follow your will because we are fearful and un-
trusting—

PEOPLE: O God, grant us new life in you.

LEADER: When we seek the security of false gods and turn our faces from
your Light—

PEOPLE: O God, grant us new life in you.

Silent Confession

Assurance of Forgiveness

LEADER: There is no greater joy in the heart of God than this moment now! For
in this moment, we call upon God to grant us new life in the center of
our wounded hearts. It is with great joy that God grants us new life
and forgiveness of our sin!

PEOPLE: In the name of Jesus Christ, we are forgiven by grace! With great joy,
we are made alive! Thanks be to God. Amen.   (JCW)

C. Prayers of Confession

1. Caring and compassionate Creator, we enter this place set apart for your worship, knowing that we have failed to see you in other places. We have ignored
your beauty around us, in earth and sky, in plants and creatures, in the people
who surround us. We have chosen to live more by our fears than by our faith, to
be weighed down by what we do not have, rather than rejoicing in your gifts to
us. In these moments together, draw us so close that we cannot help but know
every day that you are with us, wherever we go. Enlarge our capacity to care, so
we may see you in all whom we meet. In Jesus' name. Amen.   (LB)

2. O God of watchful care, you have offered us, and our ancestors before us,
your life-giving presence, yet we do not always respond. Your abundance over-
whelms us; your faithfulness confounds us, and we draw back. You have shown
us in Jesus of Nazareth the humanity you have long hoped could be ours. It
sounds so good—freedom, justice, and peace—but it asks so much of us! And
forgetting to rely on the help of your Spirit, we grow discouraged or indifferent
too easily.

And yet, we do want what you want—a new creation where we shall live,
one and all, as your children. So let this newness now be in us! Forgive what lies
behind us and turn our hearts and hands to what is ahead. Free us from the
chains of guilt and self-pity which hinder our energy to love and our ability to be
loved. Refresh our hope and vision as your church and renew our commitment
to the many ministries in which we serve. May we nurture one another as we
share the mystery of life and the proclamation of the gospel! This we pray, trusting in you, transforming God! Amen.   (ABD)

3. O God, our God, we celebrate the new life which you have given us. We
have experienced broken lives made whole, old wounds of alienation healed over,

and tired spirits rejuvenated with new vision. Gracious God, we are so grateful for the purpose and possibilities you have placed before us. Yet there are times when doubt has overcome hope, cynicism has replaced dedication, the world's values have captured us more than yours. Forgive us those times, we pray. Help us let go of the past that we might move joyfully into a new future that points to your love and justice. Amen. (LME)

4. Eternal God, from the beginning of time you have called your children into communion with you. Yet we confess that like all the rest, we have turned to our own way and refused your love and grace. Restore us to the joy of knowing you, and of recognizing your reign among us, through Jesus Christ, bringer of your good news. Amen. (RCD)

5. O God, our God, we confess that we have not always lived for you. You have invited us into new life, yet we have closed our eyes and ears and hearts against that invitation. You have shown us the way to love, yet we have chosen too often the path of uncaring. You have called us to the ministry of reconciliation, yet often we find ourselves tempted to turn away from others. You have challenged us to generosity, but many times we would rather keep to ourselves. Enter our lives, God, once again. Release us from the bonds of self-centeredness. Create in us a renewed openness to your love, that we may share your love with others. Amen. (LME)

6. Eternal God, you love us steadfastly, but we have trouble loving in return; you call us, but we have wax-filled ears; you reveal yourself, but our eyelids are heavy; you lead us toward our neighbor, but we build walls around ourselves; you hate evil, injustice, and alienation, but we get used to it. O God, we pray, help us to see ourselves both as we are and as we might be before you, and draw us by your Spirit's tether into your forgiving, renewing, and serviceable grace, through the mercies of Christ. Amen. (DBB)

7. O God, we come to you as little children who both honor and fear their parents. You are like a Mother and Father to us, so we come to you with both trust and anxiety. It has been so easy to choose the path of our own indulgence instead of the way of sacrifice. We like to feel comfortable and secure rather than risking the disfavor of others or the consequences of standing up against wrong. Forgive us, God, for being so unsure of you and of our own best selves. Grant us courage to follow the truth you reveal to us. Amen. (LB)

Assurance of Forgiveness   (*Quotes Isaiah 43:1*, RSV)

God says to us: You are my chosen ones. I love you. I'm proud of you. Stand firm in your renewed commitment. Know that I have forgiven you; I call you by name; you are mine. I have entered into covenant with you and will stand by you in all times and all places. Dare to live fully the life to which I have called you. Amen. (LB)

8. Call to Confession   (*Alludes to John 14:26*, KJV, *and Acts 2:21*, RSV)

When we are in bondage, God offers to set us free. When we are poor, God in

9-29-96

Christ identifies with us and offers us riches money cannot buy. When we are lonely and discouraged, the Holy Spirit is our Comforter, pointing us beyond ourselves. Everyone who calls on God, our Creator and Parent, for help will be saved. Let us together seek the healing only God can provide.

Prayer of Confession

O God, we confess that we have not acknowledged you as the source of our successes, our substance, our selves. We have been far more ready to complain when things go wrong than to praise when all is well. We have fed our bodies a rich diet while neglecting to feed our souls. Power and wealth have assumed greater importance to us than sensitivity and service. We have allowed religious words and forms to substitute for living encounters with the persons you have called us to love.

Forgive us, compassionate Creator, and grant us the opportunity to start over again in this new week. Keep us from repeating the mistakes of the past or from new evils that could mislead or destroy. In the name of Christ, we offer our earnest prayers for pardon and deliverance. Amen.

Assurance of Forgiveness

God hears our cries and forgives all who are penitent and believing. God provides the resources for our rescue and redemption. Whoever trusts God will not be disappointed. Whoever reaches out to others in the Spirit of Christ will know the joy of God's love. You are forgiven. You are accepted. You are loved. Share these gifts. (LB)

9. (*Alludes to James 1:17,* RSV) Forgive us, gracious Giver of all good and perfect gifts, for we seek instead the riches of possessions, status, and accomplishments. Forgive us, for we fear to believe the word in Jesus Christ that you receive and love us just as we are, right now. Through your Spirit of power, and through your act of self-giving love in Jesus Christ, give us courage to center our lives in your all-sufficient grace. Amen. (RCD)

10. Gracious God, we hear you calling. You have shown us hope and you offer us courage. We come to you as people who long to walk your pathways of grace and love. But many times, God, we get discouraged by our living. We are afraid of the difficult experiences; we despair at challenges that are given to us. The roads we walk find us weary sometimes, and we let hopelessness get the best of us. Care for us on our journey, God. Help us to know that your love is always there, sustaining us, and surrounding us with care. Take our road-weary lives and transform us to be your new people, shining in the darkness. Amen.

(SEG)

11. In this maze of life, we have often run headlong in any direction which offers a faint glimmer of hope. We rush by others in our hurry to find our own way. We seldom stop to consider our beginning in your gift of life, and our future in your gift of new life. Forgive our aimless thinking, doing, and speaking.

In this maze of life, we sometimes sit in a corner alone and, unable to speak or act because we have lost all hope, we become encased in ourselves, consuming our inner life and becoming empty. Forgive our blindness to your presence as our Creator, as our Companion, and as the One who walked this way from birth through death to a resurrected life. Amen. (DRB)

12. O God, we really don't want to see the slums, the war, the poverty, the hatred, the sickness in our world or in ourselves. We are afraid to see, to think, to feel, or to care. But help us to trust, so we can really see and care, and through our experiences, rediscover the depths, the joy, as well as the pain, of our humanness. We ask in the name of Christ. Amen. (JB)

13. Brothers and sisters in Christ, there is a dimension to my life, a dark side, sin, whose specifics I cannot bear to let you know. Were any part of those hidden things identified in public I would experience pain and shame. Further, for some part of my dark side to be identified by my brothers and sisters in the church as intolerable would wound and isolate me in ways I could not bear. Forgive me but do not ask me to be specific. (KFK)

14. God, who calls us into being, we admit that we scheme and devise our own worlds of concrete and steel, of stocks and property, of social roles and names and titles, without considering what we are doing to ourselves, to one another, and to creation. The imaginations of our wills do not join yours but go their own way.

God who calls us into your future, we admit that we lack a lively and life-giving imagination. We are content with ourselves, our culture, our politics, our social structures and choose not to break into the freedom of your new creation. Not imagining what we ourselves, our neighbors, or the creation will need tomorrow, we stand inactive and helpless before the future.

Capture the imaginations of our hearts and the work of our hands, turning them from evil toward the good of your reign. Amen. (DRB)

15. (*Alludes to Luke 15:3–7*, RSV) God, our shepherd, we have strayed like lost sheep, wandering through life, far from home. Often in our wanderings we find ourselves in places where we ought not to be, trapped and unable to turn ourselves around. Hear our cries of lostness; come rescue us and be our guide.

At other times, through fear, we huddle in the safety of the fold; not daring to venture out into your pastures where we're called to live in freedom. Come challenge us and be our guide. Amen. (MAM/DRB)

16. (*Alludes to James 1:17*, RSV) Endless source of every good and perfect gift, with you is life and the joy of living. But we forget and search everywhere for gifts that only you can give; thus we fall into sin and despair. Still you accept us; you even give us the task of leading others to the waters of life. Forgive us, and make us channels of your grace, through Jesus our Christ. Amen.
(RCD)

17. We come to you today confessing our self-centeredness. We know that we love to talk about ourselves. Our favorite topic is "I . . ." We are quite taken

with our own personal sufferings and pet grudges. Sometimes, God, we talk to people and genuinely need their comfort and support. Other times, we talk for the sake of filling airspace. We bore other persons to death with tales of our aches, our complaints, our unjust treatment. Forgive us, God. Help us to catch ourselves when we sin by inflicting our tedious selves on others. Amen.

(HWW)

18. O God, we confess to you that we do not prepare ourselves to hear your voice. We know that we are rarely attuned to you. We admit that you could shout loudly and we still might not listen to your words. We know that we don't pray often enough. We say we don't have time. We confess that we want immediate results. If we wax the floor, it looks shiny right away. If we sweep the basement, the sawdust vanishes. We are impatient if we don't get results this quickly from our praying. Forgive us, O God. Help us to learn that allowing ourselves to trust you takes time and effort on our part. We pray these things in your name. Amen. (HWW)

19. O God, there are times we don't know what to say to ourselves, or to you. What is the truth of our lives we are too scared to see; too proud to share? Prod us gently, yet insistently, to look at ourselves with honesty. We are complex creatures; our lives confused and overrun; our spirits crippled; our responses to larger issues lame.

Help us to clear the garbage away, to see clearly and hear plainly. Loosen the particular bond which fetters each of us, that we may straighten up—unwind—find movement possible once again toward you, toward ourselves, toward others. Amen. (ME)

20. Gracious God, you call us to wilderness places to plant your seeds of love there. You send us to people that need our care. You promise always to uphold us and to lead us. But we don't always listen to you. We complain that we don't know how, or we aren't good enough to talk to anyone, or that we don't get enough out of what we're doing. Free us from these notions, God. Give us the chance to bear good fruit as we live in your loving Spirit. Amen. (SEG)

21. God of love, you offer us your world and your care, and we abandon you. You welcome strangers among us, and we become jealous of them. You give us possibilities for peace and justice, and we turn them aside. We are like lost children, God. Sometimes we run from you and we hardly know our way back. Yet there you are, welcoming us, always ready to open your arms to us. Thank you, God, for being there. Amen. (SEG)

22. Powerful, gentle God, you can take desert waste and make it grow into fruitful land. We need your power to change life. Our lives are so often full of drudgery. Often we forget to live thankful lives, and we get bogged down in self-pity and blame. Empower us, God. Help us to feel your Spirit changing us, each day, that our lives may be full and glowing in your love. Through the Spirit, whose breath sustains us, we pray. Amen. (SEG)

23. God who gives, we have not always been a giving people. You give us cour-

age, and we back away in fear. Your compassion greets us warmly, and we greet one another with cold, distant stares. You touch us in mercy, and we often refuse to share our grace with anyone. Take our isolated, lonely lives, and set us free in your loving. Help us to tear down the walls of greed, and build hope in their place. Change the water of our tears into the sweet wine of your gracious love. Stay with us, God, and make us new. Through the Spirit flowing through us, we pray. Amen. (SEG)

24. God of great giving, we confess that we hoard our gifts. You give us talents of speaking and teaching, and we pretend we can't use them. You give us gifts of working with our hands and minds, and we often use those gifts for our own gain and self-satisfaction, forgetting the needs of others. You give us wisdom and knowledge, and we hide what we know, for fear of being laughed at or ignored. Open our hearts, great God, so that we can be part of your love for the world, sharing what we have. Amen. (SEG)

25. Merciful God, you show us your care in so much of life around us. You invite us into your great life of love. But often we refuse your invitation, and turn away from your call. Instead of asking you for help when we need it, we rely on our own stubborn wills. Instead of knocking at the doors of your people, we shut up our lives and hide from one another. Instead of seeking you in the faces of our sisters and brothers, we pretend not to see the need and want around us. Deliver us, great God. Show us the new life that gives us the courage to live in peace and grace. Amen. (SEG)

26. God of Grace, you are always more ready to forgive our shortcomings than we are willing to admit them. You give us great promise for our living, and we laugh at you, thinking that we are no good. You call us to difficult and inspiring missions, and we busy ourselves with other things that we decide are more important. You challenge us to have courage, and we shrink back, locking ourselves into the safety of our own homes. Bring us new life, God, so that the spirit of Christ may shine in us. Amen. (SEG)

27. God of everlasting mercy, hear our prayer today, as we bring our lives before you. We come as people who dwell on the past. We want to face your new day with life and hope in our hearts, but many times the events of our own lives weigh us down. We forget to forgive one another. We dwell on our own past mistakes. We refuse to bury dead issues and worn-out memories. Free us, free us from ourselves, God, so that we might walk your new pathways, alive with grace, through Jesus Christ. Amen. (SEG)

28. Gracious God, who made the covenant promise with our ancestors, we gather here today a rebellious people. We want to act out your intentions for us, but we keep getting mixed up by all the glitter of the world around us. You tell us to honor creation, and we use other people and animals and plant life only to meet our daily wants. You offer daily bread to every living creature, and we steal that bread from our brothers and sisters in the name of our greed. You promise us new life, and we shrink back from it in fear. Heal us, God, lest we destroy ourselves. We need your presence among us. Amen. (SEG)

29. Loving God, you give us the new commandment to love one another. But we don't always obey your words to us. So often, we get caught up in the petty arguments of love and we forget about the people who hurt because of our selfishness. Many times, we don't claim your love for us, and then we become jealous people, unaware of other people who may need our love. Free us, God. Take our weary lives and fill them with your care. We can't live without you. Through Jesus, who always managed to love us. Amen. (SEG)

30. God, you have given us the power of imagination, through which the future grasps our lives today. You have sent your prophets and set them afire with visions of human life as you intend it. Yet we confess that we have chosen other stories, replacing hope with despair, substituting comfort for holy restlessness, masking the truth rather than facing reality. Forgive us, and give us courage, that we may we drawn into the future toward the new world you are creating through Jesus the Christ. Amen. (RCD)

31. You give us a vision of a new world, O God, yet we find it so easy to abide in the old. You promise your presence among us, yet we seek our own way out of life's wilderness. Wipe away our fear of the unknown, and our obsession with the known. Make us a pilgrim people, in Jesus' name. Amen. (BHG)

32. (*Alludes to Hebrews 12:2*, RSV) Almighty God, whose eternal rule is ever present but always beyond us, claim our lives. Give us grace to live as your children in this world, which does not yet fully honor you or your Christ, yet where your Spirit is powerfully at work; through Jesus Christ, the first pioneer of your righteous realm. Amen. (RCD)

D. Assurances

1. LEADER: Through Christ, Life has been given to us as a new gift for today.
   PEOPLE: We are a new and different people from this moment on!
   LEADER: Arise then! And walk in the Light of Christ! (SEG)

2. LEADER: In Christ, we are given new life.
   PEOPLE: The old is gone away. The new is before us.
   LEADER: We are freed to live fully in the present.
   PEOPLE: That's the good news that sets us free to love! (SEG)

3. LEADER: God has called us and will lead us, even in the wilderness places.
   PEOPLE: Through Christ, we trust that God loves us and will always be with us.
   LEADER: Arise then, people of God! We are free.
   PEOPLE: Our future is open, in the living love of our Redeemer! Praise be to God. (SEG)

4. LEADER: We are the precious people of Christ.
   PEOPLE: We carry with us the special promise of God that we are loved.
   LEADER: Each day is new.

PEOPLE: The future is open.
LEADER: Let us bring free and joyful hearts before God.   (SEG)

5. LEADER: Hear the good news! God has forgiven each one of us and calls us to take our parts in the drama of redeeming love.
   PEOPLE: Praise God, who accepts and uses our very human lives in the unfolding story of salvation and new life!   (RCD)

6. The God whom we know in Jesus Christ is a God of mercy and love. When we are disillusioned with others and ourselves, God still accepts us as we are and continually moves toward us with forgiveness and comfort. We are freed by God's love to live in the freshness of each new day; we are freed to reach out to one another in a community of sympathy and joy. For these great gifts of love, let us stand and sing praise. 9-29-96   (MAN)

7. God promises us that in the midst of our brokenness and our failures, there are signs of wholeness, hope, and resurrection. The stories we share with one another in faith tell of God's work in us—changing despair and depression into awareness, breaking down the walls that divide, healing wounds of the spirit, creating the power to live in new ways and the joy to live fully. In gratitude for this great love, let us stand and sing praise.   (MAN)

8. God's love is boundless and reaches into the unknown and distant places of the earth. But it is also an intimate love which touches us in the hidden fears and *11-17-96* joys of our own lives. Be assured that God's love is present for you in the caring of this community and in the offering of Jesus' life, death, and resurrection. Be assured that the ways of God's love are still surprising and mysterious and are at work in you and among us all. For this awesome love, let us stand and sing praise.   (MAN)

9. The good news in Christ is that God offers us life at every moment, forgiving us, and inviting us to the freshness of new beginnings. Let us praise this God of grace!   (RCD)

10. All things are possible with God. Even we can be taught to hear and to see and to have the courage to live under God's reign.   (MLS)

11. (*Paraphrases Isaiah 6:3, 8, RSV*)   7-21-96
    LEADER: Holy, holy, holy is our God.
    PEOPLE: The whole earth is filled with God's glory.
    LEADER: We know our many shortcomings;
    PEOPLE: We know how thoroughly we fall short of God's glory.
    LEADER: Yet even as we recognize our faults, we find courage,
    PEOPLE: We are forgiven, we are made strong,
    LEADER: So that when God asks, "Who shall I send to do my will?,"
    PEOPLE: We will reply, "Here am I. Send me."   (MSG)

12. (*Alludes to John 2:1–11, RSV*)
    LEADER: Our God sets captives free.
    PEOPLE: We are free in God's sight.

LEADER: Our God brings new life to the desperate.
PEOPLE: We can face the new day with courage.
LEADER: Our God changes water into wine.
PEOPLE: Even our lives can change and be changed in hope. Alleluia!
Amen. (SEG)

Unison Prayers

A. *Our Common Prayer* (A paraphrase of the Lord's Prayer)

God, you are life for us,
Holy be your name.
Your new day come,
Your will be done,
On earth as in heaven.
Give us this day our bread for the morrow;
And forgive us our sins, as we forgive those who sin against us.
Strengthen us in the time of test,
And deliver us from evil.
For the power and the splendor and the fulfillment are yours,
   Now and forever. Amen. (DBR/JCN)

B. *Unison Prayers*

The Journey of Faith

1. *(Alludes to Psalm 84:6,* JB; *paraphrases the hymn "God of Grace and God of Glory" by H.E. Fosdick)*
Faithful God, we thank you that when we walk close to you in this earthly pilgrimage, the valley of the weeper becomes a place of springs. We thank you for all those who walked in faith before us, acting in courage and seeking your ways. Grant us wisdom and courage for the living of these days; through the grace of Jesus Christ. Amen. (RCD)

Stewardship

2. Grant, O God, that we may be faithful stewards of all that you have entrusted to us. May humanity exercise dominion over the earth, not to exploit or abuse, but to see that your will be done. Through the stewardship of your people, may you look once more at your creation and say, "It is good," through the grace of Jesus Christ. Amen. (RCD)

Self-giving

3. Compassionate God, when we contemplate the self-giving love of Jesus, it makes us realize how much we need to grow. Come to us, and purify us with the

fire of your Spirit, that we may praise you forever and walk in your ways, through Jesus Christ, the Sovereign One. Amen. (RCD)

Music

4. O God who has called us into this congregation in common devotion to you with a variety of gifts, hear us as we dedicate this work to you. Thank you for the gift of music, the lilt of song; thank you that you have set some to sing, some to play instruments, and some to savor the notes in the silences of their beings. Thank you for the rich gift of music in our congregation. Hallelujah! Amen.

(KFK)

New Life

5. Gracious One, we give you thanks for the hope that is ours in Jesus Christ. We thank you that you forgive us and give us power to begin anew. Therefore we pray that you will come to us and touch those secret places in our lives that we most need to change. Tear down the barriers that keep us from loving others. Root out all violence from our lives. Free us from dependency on any person or thing or substance, that we may place our full trust in you. Instill us with discipline to establish new habits. Teach us to care for our bodies. Prune away the dead leaves of our lives; through your creative power, may new shoots come forth from the barren stem. Bring forth your new life within us, through the grace of Jesus Christ. Amen. (RCD)

Suffering

6. Gracious and compassionate God, we know you do not will that any should suffer needlessly. Yet confronted by suffering in our own lives and the lives of others, there are many questions we cannot answer. Help us to find peace by resting in your love; teach us to be patient with all that is unresolved within us. Teach us your compassion, that we might not hurt others thoughtlessly, but instead bring light and hope; in the name of Jesus, the suffering Servant Messiah, we pray. Amen. (RCD)

Justice for Women

7. O Most Holy God, many among us fail to feel the ways in which words, titles, and phrases oppress the inner identity and emerging self of many women.

We pray that your church may be freed from insensitivity to the power of words and actions that bind women to economic injustice, sexual abuse, and emotional injury.

May we become a people who truly live out in both our actions and our language a life-style of equality, mutual respect, and appreciation for our uniqueness. Amen. (JH)

In Time of Despair

8. Holy Comforter, be with us in those seasons when we wander from the path of joy into the winter of our spiritual life. Be our light when we experience a time of trial or tribulation, a time of loneliness or despair, a time of question or

doubt. May the pathways of Christ reopen avenues for new life and celebration. Amen. (JH)

Trust in Uncertain Times

9. Generous God, you grant us bread for our bodies and grace that is renewed every day. In these uncertain times, help us to trust you more fully, living one day at a time, loving and serving as we can. Cheer our hearts with the knowledge that we are precious to you, through Jesus our Christ. Amen. (RCD)

Need for God

10. O God of great compassion, we come to you with hopeful and trusting hearts. In our spoken words and in our deepest thoughts, we lift up to you the needs of ourselves and the world. Sometimes out of necessity, sometimes out of desperation, we have taken to beds of pain and fear. Our soreness aches for your touch. Our guilt longs for your mercy. Our dis-ease seeks your healing. Vibrant Spirit of Life, come and raise us up! Blow like spring wind through the stale spaces of our being and send us on our way renewed. In every experience, through every distress of mind and body, keep us ever mindful that your presence with us, O God, is our greatest health and true salvation. Amen.

(ABD)

Autumn 9-28-96

11. Dear God, thank you for the changing of seasons. Forgive us when we complain that winter is too cold or summer is too hot, or that we don't like the wind and cool rains of spring. Help us to remember beautiful autumn. May our lives be like an autumn tree, always growing upward to heaven, branches reaching out to God, leaves falling like our years. Amen. (BS)

Winter (Paraphrases a line from the hymn "All Beautiful the March of Days" by F.W. Wile, and Psalm 139:1–6, 13–15, RSV)

12. Great Creator of the rose and the crystal of the snow, you are our creator as well. You who knit us together in our mothers' wombs, you know us through and through, and still you love us. How wonderful is all that you do! How amazing is your care for all creation! Help us to trust in you, during these dark days of winter, with our whole selves. Make us courageous to live as your people. Through Jesus Christ we pray. Amen. (RCD)

Trust

13. O God, most loving Parent, we thank you that you are not a faraway God, hidden in magnificence in the heavens; we thank you that you commune with us in the depths of our souls. You know us through and through; you hear our prayers; you heal our sorrows. Like a father, you pity us; like a mother, you comfort us. Help us to live in childlike trust in you, that we may be free to live with courage as your children on earth. Amen. (RCD)

Freedom

14. God of our lives, to whom our stories are as important as those of persons who have gone before us, help us to learn from their experiences and to value our own. Help us to understand that your Word is one of communion and not of domination; of welcome and not of exclusion; of liberation to new life, and not of oppression in old roles. We thank you that in Christ you have given us this good news of hope and release from bondage and despair. We pray in the name of Jesus Christ, who is our freedom. Amen.   (BP)

Discipleship

15. *(Quotes the United Church of Christ Statement of Faith)*   Gracious God, you call us into your church to accept the cost and joy of discipleship. Help us to understand and accept the costs of following Christ, that we may know the joy you intend for the faithful. Make us lifelong learners in the school of faithfulness, through Jesus Christ. Amen.   (RCD)

Faith

16. Forgiving and accepting God, you who believe more in us than we do in ourselves: increase our faith in you and in ourselves, that we may serve you and the world you have made with confidence and courage, so we may accomplish your will and fulfill our own lives. In Jesus' name we pray. Amen.   (RWD)

God's Presence

17. Creating God, who brought us into this world, breathed your Spirit into us, and endowed us with your likeness: we give thanks to you for our creation and for the cords of love that bind us and nourish us in the community you have created. We pray for your continued presence to feed and sustain us as a family you have formed and which bears your name. This we ask in the name of Jesus Christ. Amen.   (RWD)

C. Introductions to Silent Prayer

1. If you have ever watched a flock of birds resting or feeding, you may have noticed a remarkable thing. When the time comes to take flight, even though no sound is made, the multitude of birds takes off and sets its course as a unit. It is as if the many are unified and directed by some unspoken purpose. In our time of silence, let us reflect on our purpose as a flock and make ourselves receptive to the unspoken guidance of God. Perhaps in doing this we will come closer and closer to flying in unity in God's direction . . . *(Silence)*   (GER)

2. Times of prayer remind me a great deal of something important I discovered one day in my childhood. Let me explain. . . . A friend and I used to play at an abandoned sandpit near his house. It was a terrific place for making noise because if you shouted from the rim of the pit toward the woods, there was a subtle echo

back. Nothing distorted, just a distinct, satisfying echo. So whenever we went there we made lots of noise (being normal, rowdy kids playing hard, heroic games). But one day as we sat on the rim, one of us asked, "Whaddya wanna do?" and the other said, "Let's just sit and listen for a change." We did. We heard birdsongs, rustling weeds, even the sand itself sliding down the pit-slope. The sandpit we knew so well took on a special newness.

Sometimes our times of prayer can be too much our noise and too little our listening. In the next few moments of silence, let your spirits become as prayerful listeners . . . *(Silence)* (GER)

3. Families are special. Often, family members can communicate with one another in wordless ways. I remember silent family times when there was a great deal being said . . . sitting around the fireplace in the evening, feeding ducks at a county park, waiting for an operation on Mom or Dad to be over, walking together to church. Sometimes words don't need to be spoken out loud for feelings to be understood. As members of God's family we can be sure that we're heard and understood even when our prayer is, as now, silent. *(Silence)*

(GER)

For Springtime

4. This is the season when many of us are trying to coax beautiful and edible things from the ground. Gardens become places for both exertion and relaxation. But for all our noisy efforts the growth of plants comes, I like to think, in silent times when the ground cradles a seed and nudges it awake, when sun-energy prompts spurts of tender shoots, when the rain delivers delicious soil-juices to thirsty roots. In the growth we rejoice . . . and brag to neighbors . . . and appreciate the miracle.

We, too, grow in silent times. And the miracle of these moments of prayer is that God nourishes us, enlightens us, and comforts us. . . . Entering the time with appreciative spirits, let us pray. (GER)

Litanies

1. *(Paraphrases Psalms 61:1–4 and 62:5, RSV)*
   ALL: Hear our cry, O God, and listen to our prayer.
   LEADER: From the ends of the earth, we call to you.
   PEOPLE: Hear our cry, O God.
   LEADER: Lead us to new life and to high ground.
   PEOPLE: Hear our prayer, O God.
   LEADER: Let us be safe under the shelter of your protective wing.
   PEOPLE: Make us whole, we pray.
   LEADER: For you alone, O God, our souls wait, and our lives are spent in
            service;
   PEOPLE: Hear our longing, O God.

LEADER: Listening for you in the beauty and wonder of creation,
PEOPLE: We hear you, God of love, and we are yours. Amen. (RDS)

2. Opening Words of Praise and Confession

LEADER: We gather today to praise God who created all things, cares for us tenderly, and calls each of us to a life of service and ministry.
PEOPLE: Let us give praise for God's gifts of life, love, and meaningful work.
LEADER: We also gather today to confess our failure to be the people God has created us to be.
ALL: O God, we are a wayward people. Too often we hear your call only to ignore it. We take perverse pleasure in destroying what you have created. We seek our selfish interests, personal pleasure, and short-term gains. We become enslaved by our desire for security. Forgive our lack of vision. Take away our stubbornness and our greed. Lead us in your ways, we pray, for your sake. Amen. (VSS)

3. Litany of the Sower *(The parable of the sower is found in Mark 4:3–9, RSV, and parallels; also alludes to Deuteronomy 7:6, RSV)*

LEADER: In the parable of the sower we are both the soil and the sower; we both receive from God and we give out the Word. What kind of soil are we?
PEOPLE: We are soil which sometimes is hard. We crack under the hardness, and the seeds of new life have no home in us. There is no place for God's Word to take root and grow within our lives. Instead, what we hear is easily forgotten, and we neglect the Words of Life.
LEADER: But are we all one kind of soil, and each of us always the same?
PEOPLE: No. We are also the soil that grows thistles and bristles at times, Our thorny selves strangle the Word of Life before it can grow within us and around us.
LEADER: Again I ask, could we be yet another kind of soil?
PEOPLE: Yes, sometimes we are a very rich and fertile soil that receives the seed of Life, and it grows in us. At times our lives are receptive to God's Word, and all kinds of people, and all kinds of soil. We are sometimes people like those of whom Jesus says, "And some of the seed fell into good soil, where it bore fruit." We seek to be a people who bear the fruit of Life in Christ; we seek to sow among all people the words and acts which show God's love and justice, that divine mercy and truth.
LEADER: Ah, so we are both the soil and sower; and many kinds of both. As the soil we will receive the seeds of Life, the Word. As the sower, we will give out those Words of Life to other people. In doing this we experience the breaking forth of joy in our lives. For joy does break forth among the people of God who have ears to hear, for God says, "For you are a people holy to God." Serve God, and sing, all you people who do the will of God in your lives.

(BJW)

4. Litany of Thanksgiving   (*Quotes Philippians 3:20,* RSV)

LEADER: As chicks gathered beneath the Mother Hen,
PEOPLE: We are sustained by the gentle care of Christ through our sisters and brothers.
LEADER: As imitators of Paul and the apostles,
PEOPLE: We live as friends of the cross.
LEADER: As citizens of the world whose commonwealth is in heaven,
PEOPLE: We await a savior, Jesus the Christ.
LEADER: As Christians in worship and in work,
PEOPLE: We rejoice in God.   (DRB)

Litanies and Prayers Based on Psalms

1. A Psalm (*Inspired by Psalms 78 and 107 and based on ideas from the Adult Class, Bethel-Bethany UCC, Milwaukee*)

Thanks to God, who is good:
There were those who were held hostage in a strange land: You found them in the foreign places and led them home.
There were those who struggled all of every day just to eat and drink; the eyes of their children cried out in need and their bellies stretched out for help:
You offered your chosen people the opportunity to give food and drink in Jesus' name, and they did.
There were those who ached in body and mind, who waited in needy silence or called out in pain:
You offered skills to your servants to heal the sick in body and soul, and they did.
There were those who were blown up beyond their own height, and you brought them down to earth;
There were those who were ashamed to their very foundation, and you lifted them up to the mountaintop;
There were those whose sorrows seemed never-ending; they cried out in the midst of the city:
And you gave them comfort like a quiet garden, serenity like a placid lake.
We build walls of protective security with bricks of fear and hate; we call out for a trumpet to tumble down our Jerichos;
You send us Wisdom, who teaches us how to take down the walls, brick by brick.
When we ask for forgiveness for our failures, you send us Christ, to free us from our sin.
When we ask that our desires be satisfied, you send us the Way, setting us free to love and serve.
When we ask, you answer with the Word.
Let us give thanks to God.   (RAF)

2. A Responsive Affirmation (*Based on Psalm 46:1–2*, RSV)

LEADER: God is our refuge and our strength,
PEOPLE: A very present help in trouble.
LEADER: Therefore we will not fear though the earth should change.
PEOPLE: Therefore we are not lost, even though we wander.
LEADER: God is our refuge and our strength.   (MSG)

3. American Psalm

Look upon this land, O God;
    behold the achievement of your people America.
From early days we carried your word;
    we sang your song as we cleared the wilderness.
Royalty across the sea scoffed at the rebels in buckskin;
    learned ones scorned our preachers on horseback.
Now the whole earth gazes in envy,
    both the weak and the mighty seek our shores.

O God, the warehouses are full,
    the storage shelves bend with weight.
The merchants' appeals are a wonder to all peoples,
    their songs are on our lips.
Scraps from our tables amaze the hungry;
    heaps of discards tower above us.
Vehicles pass in endless parade.
    The murmur of the highway is a lullaby.

Yet voices assail us from every side;
    headlines warn of tomorrow's sorrows.
They ask whether dead fish swim and spawn
    or the unemployed laugh.
The fields hold but a handsbreadth of topsoil,
    the rest is gone in the air and the water.
What do we owe for days of plenty?
    We have planted chemicals and grown poisons.
Our enemies remind us of the mushroom shadow
    that hides the sun,
And our children are dismayed;
    their sleep is consumed by dreams of a broken future.

When everything is gone,
    in the cold silence you are there;
Before and after,
    you alone.
Which of the empires has endured?
    Israel is only a remnant.
Yet alongside the ghost of greatness
    an upright people might stand.

Save us, O God of Salvation!
Draw near to us, that we may be restored!

Praise be to God!   (DLM)

Offertory

Offertory Sentence

(*Quotes Matthew 5:7*, RSV)   Jesus said, "Blessed are the merciful, for they shall obtain mercy."

May our morning offering be an act of gratitude given from a merciful heart.   (RNE)

Offering Prayers

1. (*Alludes to Isaiah 9:2*, RSV)   May these gifts bring light to those who walk in darkness, hope to those who live in despair, and justice to those who are oppressed. Grant to each giver a sense of participation in the most important opportunity of all time: to share your love with the world. To this end, we dedicate our offerings and ourselves. Amen.   (LB)

2. One and Eternal God of time and space, we respond to you with joy as we lift up our tithes and offerings. The opportunity to share is a blessing for which we are very thankful. Your generous provision for our needs prompts us to be generous in return. Accomplish your purposes, we pray, through these gifts and in our lives. Amen.   (LB)

3. Through our offerings we identify with the cause of Christ. We proclaim our concern for all people, and name them as our own next-of-kin. We identify with their suffering and grief and we rejoice when good comes to them. Both our material resources and our personal time and effort are offered here to extend the body of Christ into this moment in history and into the whole world. Amen.
(LB)

4. Our spiritual ancestors offered sacrifices to glorify you, O God; so would we honor you by these gifts. May they express the depth of our love for you. As your church, we put them to work on your behalf in programs of outreach toward those who long for meaning as well as for life's other necessities. Grant your joy to all who give and all who receive. Amen.   (LB)

5. Thank you, God, for the opportunity to share in your creative and restorative work among people. Because you have blessed us, we have much to give. These offerings express our gratitude and our aspiration to be more fully your own loyal community. Amen.   (LB)

6. We bring these offerings because of the love you have poured out on us in the life, death, and resurrection of Jesus. Your gift calls for a response that cannot be

contained in envelopes or baskets. Nothing less than all we have and all we are is good enough to dedicate to your will and purposes. With fear and trembling, yet with joy, relief, and gratitude, we bring you all we have to give—ourselves. Use us, that your rule may be realized among all people. Amen. (LB)

7. Your importance in our lives, O God, is reflected in our gifts. We return to you, through the ministry and outreach of this church, a portion of all you have entrusted to us. We promise that these offerings will not be the end of our giving. We will also invest our time and abilities in your work of healing, comforting, teaching, guiding, and proclaiming good news. Bless each gift, whatever its size, and multiply the good to be done through our time, talents, and treasure. Amen. (LB)

8. We offer ourselves with our gifts, confident that you have a purpose for them and for us. Expand our limited vision to embrace new possibilities. We rededicate our lives at this altar. May our offerings reach beyond the barriers of our former thinking and doing. In the Spirit of Christ, we would pray and live.
(LB)

9. For every benefit we praise you, God; for every gift received and for each gift we are blessed in giving. For all your goodness we give thanks to you: the providence which made and nourishes life; the presence which brings meaning in divine and human love, and the promise that gives hope for each new moment. Out of faith and into hope we are led by your love, and for these graces we return our thanks, through the mercies of Jesus Christ. Amen. (DB)

10. (*Alludes to 1 Corinthians 1:18*, RSV)   For those who are being saved, the cross is no longer folly. Therefore, we present our gifts before this symbol of sacrifice and service. We seek to share the story of suffering love that fulfills life and conquers death. Bless these gifts and all who give; use our wealth, our time, our abilities for the good of all your people. Amen. (LB)

Statements of Faith

1. We know that God is in the world—was and is and will be. God made it all, and continues to renew and remake and resurrect.

We know God best in the life of Jesus, who was and is our maker of hope, the one who saves.

We know the power and energy of God in the Holy Spirit.

We are filled with God's joy and pledged to discipleship and love.

We trust in God. We celebrate God. We work together for justice and peace through God.

We are never alone. We are free in the chosen bonds of the ways of the Christ. Thanks be to God! (MSG/RDS)

2.   We are the People of God.

We are a sign of the New World.

We are the sisters and brothers of Jesus.

We believe in God. We believe in the goodness of God, the presence of God in human history, and the nearness of God's love.

We believe in Christ. We believe that God was and is revealed in human life, that out of human suffering may come rescue and healing, that out of death comes new life.

We believe in the Eternal Spirit, who moves among God's people and invites the world into God's reign. We believe that the world can change, that peace and wholeness can come, and that the New World can arrive.

We are the people of God.

We are the sign of the New World.

We are the brothers and sisters of Jesus.

(DB)

Benedictions

A. Scriptural Benedictions (RCD)

1. (*1 Thessalonians 3:11–13*, RSV, *abridged*)   Now may our God make you to increase in love to one another and to all people and establish your hearts unblamable in holiness.

2. (*2 Thessalonians 2:16–17*, RSV, *abridged*)   Now may . . . God . . . who loved us and gave us eternal comfort and good hope through grace, comfort your hearts and establish them in every good word and work.

3. (*Philippians 4:4–7*, RSV, *adapted*)   Rejoice in the Lord Jesus Christ always. Again, I say, rejoice. Do not be anxious about anything, but in all things by prayer and supplication with thanksgiving let your requests be made known to God. And the peace of God which passes all understanding will keep your hearts and minds in Christ Jesus.

4. (*Philippians 1:9–11*, RSV, *adapted*)   May your love abound more and more, with knowledge and all understanding, so that you may approve what is excellent, and pure and blameless for the day of Christ, filled with the fruits of righteousness which come through Jesus Christ, to the glory and praise of God.

5. (*Ephesians 3:20–21*, RSV, *adapted*)   And now to the God who by the power at work within us is able to do far more abundantly than all that we ask or think, be glory in the church and in Christ Jesus to all generations, for ever and ever. Amen.

6. (*Galatians 5:22–23, 25*, RSV)   The fruit of the Spirit is love, joy, peace, patience, kindness, goodness, faithfulness, gentleness, self-control. If we live by the Spirit, let us also walk by the Spirit.

7. *(2 Corinthians 5:17, RSV, adapted, with additional material)*   If any one is in Christ, that person is a new creation. The old has passed away; behold, the new has come. Walk in the newness of life. God is with you. Amen.

8. *(Romans 16:25, 27, RSV, adapted)*   Now to the One who is able to strengthen you according to the gospel and the preaching of Jesus Christ . . . to the only wise God, be glory forevermore through Jesus Christ. Amen.

9. *(Romans 15:13, RSV)*   May the God of hope fill you with all joy and peace in believing, so that by the power of the Holy Spirit you may abound in hope. Amen.

10. *(Paraphrases 2 Corinthians 13:14, KJV)*   The love of God, the grace of Jesus Christ, and the communion of the Holy Spirit be and abide with you all. Amen.

11. *(1 Peter 3:9, RSV, adapted, with additional material)*   You are a chosen race, a royal priesthood, a holy nation, God's own people, that you may declare the wonderful deeds of God who called you out of darkness into marvelous light. Go into the world; live as God's people, through the grace of Jesus Christ and the power of the Holy Spirit. Amen.

12. *(Romans 15:5, RSV, adapted)*   May the God of steadfastness and encouragement grant us to live in such harmony with one another, in accord with Jesus Christ, that together we may glorify God now and forever. Amen.

13. *(Hebrews 13:20, RSV, adapted)*   Now may the God of peace, who brought again from the dead Jesus, the great shepherd of the sheep, by the blood of the everlasting covenant, equip you with everything good, that you may do what is pleasing in God's sight, through Jesus Christ, to whom be glory forever and ever. Amen.

14. *(1 Thessalonians 5:14–23, RSV, abridged and adapted)*   Encourage the fainthearted; help the weak; be patient with all; seek to do good; rejoice always; pray without ceasing; give thanks in all circumstances. And so may the God of peace sanctify you wholly; and may your spirit and soul and body be kept sound at the coming of Jesus Christ. Amen.

B. Pastoral Benedictions

1. *(After a music service)*   God, we thank you for the gift of music, for the rich inspiration of past ages, and for the loveliness that gives life meaning. Send us forth, humming the great melodies that have become the hymns of faith. Send us forth inspired, that in all we do we might show Christ, the light to all the world. Amen.   (RLA)

2. Friends,
   Continue your journey walking in love.
   Care for one another, care for the earth.

Seek justice and make peace.
God goes before you.
Live boldly, celebrate and sing! (MAM)

3. God gives life. God renews life. God is life.
Celebrate the life within you and let it overflow to enliven the world.
    May the peace of God dwell within this week and forevermore. Amen.
(PM)

4. Go into the world with faith, trusting all to receive you. Go into the world
with hope—with God's will before you and great dreams in your heart. Go into
the world with love—love for all people: serving with those in whom Christ
lives and laboring for those for whom Christ died; and the faithfulness of God,
the hope which quickens God's Spirit within us, and the love of Christ be with
us all. Amen. (WRW)

5. (*Quotes Matthew 28:20*, RSV)   Jesus said: Lo, I am with you always, even
to the end of the age. Go in peace: Christ is with you. You are a dearly loved
child of God. Rejoice! (RCD)

6. Go gladly into the world. Be filled with the love of God. Dance to the song
of the Spirit. Befriend the Christ in each new day. Amen. (GER)

7. Let us greet the world as children of God, rejoicing in its wonders, sharing its
goodness with our sisters and brothers. And may the vision and reality of God's
peace make this world a happy home for all the human family. Amen.
(GER)

C. Responsive Benedictions

1. LEADER: The peace of God go with you this day, reigning within you, and in
    your families.
  PEOPLE: God's peace will make a difference in our lives, in all our relation-
    ships.
  LEADER: Walk in confident friendship with Christ, who suffers and rejoices
    with you.
  PEOPLE: Christ's presence will transform and strengthen us, wherever our
    journeys take us this week.
  LEADER: Live by the Spirit, acknowledging God's rule in your hearts and in
    your actions.
  PEOPLE: We welcome the fires of the Holy Spirit, the refreshing wind of
    God's surprising grace.
  ALL: Amen. (LB)

2. LEADER: As we have celebrated our common faith, so may you worship God
    where you are every day.
  PEOPLE: We trust God to stand by us in our struggles and help us change and
    grow.

LEADER: Look beyond the accumulation of things to those relationships with people that give life meaning.

PEOPLE: We will dare to share ourselves with all people God loves, that we may more fully understand each other.

LEADER: Hear the stories your sisters and brothers want to tell, for God may speak to you through them.

PEOPLE: We want to feel their pain and their joy, to live in mutual acceptance and peace.

LEADER: The peace of God go with you and be shared through you. Amen.

PEOPLE: Amen. (LB)

D. Sung Response After Benediction

(Tune: BUNESSAN, usually used with "Morning Has Broken")
New life has bloomed here,
God's love has warmed us;
Now the world calls us
To go and spread that love.
God's peace go with you.
May it sustain you,
And bring us together
To praise God again. (PM)

Pastoral Prayers

1. O God, make us instruments of your love . . . *(pause)*

We ask that you play the song of life through us as though we were stringed instruments. Stretch our concerns and capabilities so that the church as the body of Christ may resonate with good works. Let our individual lives be as single strings producing clear and characteristic notes of grace; forgive our tendency to let go of our true tone with changes in the climate around us. We confess that when we become less attuned to your will, joyful notes turn flat and we make noise instead of music.

O God, we long to accompany your child Jesus in the dance of life. Place your hands upon us so our sounds together might be harmonious, music that joins neighbors in chorus and that gives voice to the spritely Spirit of peace.

We await your touch as we enter worship; make us instruments of your love. In the name of Jesus Christ. Amen. (GER)

2. We seek courage to worship you with our whole selves, for to do so may change us. Move with us, shelter us, when we fear the seeming emptiness of our silence. Fill us, move us, when futility and frustration threaten to paralyze us, that we may be living, loving hands and feet: instruments of your acts.

That we may be mindful of our connectedness to you and to all creation through the Spirit, we pray

for persons in need of healing *(here the leader asks for names)*;
for leaders in need of direction *(names are requested)*;
for lives in need of caring *(names are requested)*.

O God, may the whole world today know a moment of living with purpose, enthusiasm, and courage, and may such moments grow. Amen.   (ME)

3. Most Gracious God—you who have given us the gifts which we know through the moving strains of music, through a smile and a tear, a sigh and a shout, through laughter and weeping, a prayer, silence, the beauty of such a day and place, . . . God, for these gifts and the meaning of them for each of us, know our gratitude and our expressions of praise.

We pray for the church—sometimes triumphant and present, while at other times, seeming to be failing and distant. Sometimes we are together and at-one—uniting the variety of parts that we are to include even the smallest into a whole that transcends our limits and boundaries. At other times, we are scattered and divided—torn and hurting, afraid and self-righteous. Sometimes we are truly serving, while at other times, we demand and want only to be served. Sometimes we are filled with your Spirit, which enlivens, empowers, and transforms, while at other times we are only a skeleton that settles for what is—afraid and yes, lazy. Holy One, your Spirit catches us and fills us and frees us. Help us to be your church, to appreciate the gifts which we are given and share them gratefully that there may be a stronger, serving, enlivening, empowering, and transforming body in this world—your church!

Bless, dear God, this particular congregation and the worldwide church of which we are part. Forgive us when we think of ourselves first, and forgive us for the foolish pride that we sometimes feel—both expressed openly and secretly—that ours is better, that ours is more faithful, and that ours is the way . . . while at the same time, know our gratitude for the freedom and the variety that we enjoy as members of this church.

We pray for the world—this one world in which we live—one in which there is abundance and yet limits, one in which there is food and yet hungry people, one in which there is healing and yet hurting, one in which there is peace and yet war. We pray for the world which you so love, that you sent us the Christ to believe, to trust and to follow, that there might be life and freedom forever. Yet there is unbelief. Forgive us; help us truly to believe, that by so believing, we will hope and by so hoping, we will do what needs to be done, until there is enough for all in just proportions. And, Sovereign God, may there be peace.

You know the particular concerns that lie heaviest in our hearts and minds. Receive these our silent prayers as we offer them to you . . .

In the name of Jesus. Amen.   (ARE)

4. *(After a time of silent prayer; paraphrases Romans 12:15,* RSV*)*
We thank you, compassionate God, that you hear the prayer of every heart:
those who rejoice at a baby's new birth,

those who mourn when the circle is complete and a friend or loved one has
   died,
those who are grateful when their work meets with success,
those who suffer because no work is to be found,
those who are bored, not having enough to do,
those who are tired, having too much to do,
those who are surrounded by the love of family and friends,
those who are lonely.

Thank you for hearing us in every situation of life, for we all play each of
these roles sooner or later. Help us to support one another, rejoicing with those
who rejoice, and weeping with those who weep. For we want to be joined together as members of the body of Christ, in unity loving one another and serving
the world. We want, like Jesus, to respond to each human being who crosses our
path with sensitivity and compassion. It is in the name of Jesus that we pray.
Amen.   (RCD)

5. Help us, O God, these hot summer days to find moments to turn to you. In
quietness and returning to you, be our strength. Cool the fever of overpaced
lives.

Refresh us with the gentle rain of the Spirit. Like the sound of thunder and
the sight of lightning, startle us with new opportunities to serve.

Grant us your peace. We know you are closer to us than breath, your voice
quiet and strong like a heartbeat.

Help us to be aware of your presence and to hear your voice, for your Word
is our life. Amen.   (RCD)

6. (*Alludes to Luke 15:1–32*, RSV)   Gracious God of the loving heart, by
whom all fatherhood and motherhood is named, Source of our creation, you
whose Trinity of persons all human bonding and richness of human community
reflects, may your name be praised!

God of infinite light, even incognito in our darkness, architect of this earthly
garden which is our home, divine Friend at the center of our aloneness and at the
center of our connectedness, may your name be praised!

Because of the boundlessness of your love, you opened your womb, pouring
forth your own inner life, giving birth to the world, and bestowing on it life like
your own. As a shepherd searches for sheep that are lost, so you follow us
wherever we go to bring us back to the safety of your arms. As a woman looks
into every nook and cranny to find the coin which she has lost, so you look for
us in every out-of-the-way place where we hide from you. As a father stands by
and waits, longing for his absent son and grieving for his self-righteous one, so
you wait for us until we "come to ourselves" and choose to come back to you.
You are our lifeline. Help us then to make you our life.

We pray today, especially for those who seek to care for your creation, using
all *things* as sacraments of joy, as a means of companionship with you.

For those who work with your gifts:
—who eke out a living on the land;
—who shelter its forests and respect its water;

—who measure the air, its temperature and its terrors;

—who dig deeply beneath its secrets.

And we pray for others who seek to care for your creation, seeing all *persons* as revelations of your image, as a means of sharing love with you.

For those who tend your gifts of *human* life:

—who plot the path of planes and subways to bring them safely home;

—who tend the human body by surgery, by legal rights, by filling us with good food;

—who choose to be a moral minority when the fracturing of human community tears us apart;

—who protest every instrument of terror, every bomb and missile which threatens tender life on this earth.

And we pray for ourselves, charged with stewardship over all things and all human life. Give us the grace to be patient gardeners, faithful and watchful shepherds, merciful and compassionate judges, angry dissidents, wondrous fashioners of new imaginations, and committed nurses of a thirsty and hungry world.

Fountain of life and example for us all, we offer ourselves to be a likeness of yours in whom and through whom we have been given our life, our names, and our tasks.

With the innocence and wisdom of the children of God, we join together in that prayer which Jesus taught those who claimed his name . . .   (JAP)

7. (*Written in response to Luke 6:17–26,* RSV, *the Beatitudes*)   Our God, we gather in this place, looking to you to heal our hurts and to offer us counsel. We are members of the human family: we belong to the crowd, and yet each is alone. Every distinct story, and our common human story: all are a puzzle. We are the poor and the rich, the hungry and the satisfied. Now we weep; now we laugh. The pieces of our lives, of each and of all, seem never to fit together. We await your restoring word.

And your word comes, O God, but not as we expected. Here you lift us from poverty; there you strip us of our security. Now we mourn, and you comfort; now we jest, and you cut short our easy laughter. Your word comes to humble us, with mercy and with judgment.

Our God, we are members of the human family; we are your children. To us all, give ears to hear your word of promise and challenge. To us all, bring a healing deeper than the assurances and comforts we seek. Wherever we suffer amid poverty, war, oppression; wherever we live by illusions of success, security, power:

Heal us.

Heal us, O God, by the power of your truth, for we yearn that our world be whole.

We pray, as we would live, in the name of that One whose touch is healing, whose word is truth: even Jesus Christ. Amen.   (MLP)

8. Loving God, who creates us into new be-ing each day, help us to discover your purpose for our lives and to seek our roles in fulfilling this purpose. We

2-11-96

praise you for your creation of our lives day by day, for your re-creation of hope within us, even when hope seems foolish. We pray for this world of ours, in which cynical self-interest and grasping for power often seem to be the rules by which human beings live. We confess our responsibility for those thoughts and actions by which we further the powers of evil and destruction in our world, for we know finally that becoming human is a process of reconciliation and not of separation, of trust and not of suspicion, of communion and not of coercion. We accept your call to peacemaking, wherever we may be and in whatever situation we find the hatreds, the fears, or the distrusts which cry out for peace to heal and to mend the brokenness.

Help us each to offer thanks to you, not in empty words or pious gestures, but in lives which are faithful to your call. Enable us to bear the fruits of thankfulness in serving others and in building community with the men, women, and young persons in our lives. May we reach out to these persons, supporting them in their struggles and celebrating with them their joys and victories. May we also accept the love and friendship offered to us by others, as we confess and acknowledge our needs, our weaknesses, our times of despair and hopelessness. We see your loving purpose in these expressions of human concern; we feel your loving touch healing us and caring for us as a child is cared for by a parent. Especially, today, reach out and touch ——— and ———; be with them in their time of illness and suffering. We lift up in prayer to you these friends from our congregation that you may bring healing and wholeness to their lives.

We know that you are with us and for us in the midst of our lives. We praise you for this constant love and in Jesus' name we offer together the prayer of our Savior: (BP)

9. O God whom no one has seen, yet who endlessly beholds all that you have made, we shudder to think that you see us here in our Sunday best, but know us at our weekday worst.

How splendid we are in fine clothes that bespeak the wisdom that cleanliness is next to godliness, but how shoddy we feel within.

There is the love that is betrayed,
there are the promises we have broken,
there are the things that we want to forget,
there are the ambitions that we have exchanged for cheap comfort and ease.

You who can see our selves beneath our shining shells, only you can forgive our aimlessness and sin. Have mercy upon us and help us to reclaim what is left of lives so incomplete and uncommitted.

In your presence we gather once more to hear the old, old story that is music to our ears. So easily we accept the rituals of worship, yet how quickly we protest the timely obligations that call for courage or patience or love. Upset our comfortable righteousness and drive us into the streets and marketplaces where men and women suffer and die, where children in hunger cry themselves to sleep. Lead us through the corridors of homes and hospitals where, on bed after bed, forgotten older people wait for the merciful deliverance of death. Make us one with all humanity in the longing and labor for peace.

We know, O Savior, that Christ would not pass by us or our neighbors. Grant, most gracious God, that we, too, may pass by no neighbor in need, nor fail to offer a cup of help and healing in Christ's name. Amen.   (WRW)

Special Events

A. *Litany for a Groundbreaking*

LEADER: We praise you, O God, for the joy we find in the church: for communion with one another; for the sharing of bounty and of burden; for nurturing, one generation of the next; for expressions of holiness made visible in our midst.

PEOPLE: O God, lead us in your ways through this the instrument of your church.

LEADER: We give you thanks, O God, for the strengths which have brought this day into being: the vision which came to dwell on this ground years ago; the laborers of the past whose memories we carry in our hearts; the duteous service of today's leaders who would cast tomorrow's church.

PEOPLE: O God, make us ever mindful of each person's special contribution to the life of this your church.

LEADER: We stand in awe, O God, of the wondrous skills here assembled: the encompassing eye of the planner; the tempered patience of crafter and engineer; the calloused hands of builder who labors for the common good.

PEOPLE: O God, let no talent be overlooked in the building of your reign and let us never fail to acknowledge each offering made to this your church.

LEADER: We call to you, O God, to cast your spirit among us this day. Let us be builders of a holy temple: a place where humans may find peace in the face of turmoil, yet not a place where complacency finds a home. Let us be servants and visionaries both: Planters and harvesters each, stewards of a living treasure.

PEOPLE: O God, make the seeds we plant this day call forth a bounteous crop and let the fruit of that crop be our lives dedicated to you now and ever more. Amen.   (DRK)

B. *Covenant for the Installation of a Pastor*

We the members of _____ affirm our call to ministry in the name of Jesus Christ. As ones named to be God's emissaries we accept these charges:

to gather in common worship and assure that the doors of this meetinghouse may be open to all who seek spiritual nurture,

to sustain one another when burdened,

to extend the hand of charity,
to loose the bonds of bigotry, malice, hatred, and ill-will,
to share the good news of God's love in deed and in word,
to seek knowledge, that each generation may grow in wisdom.

Committed to these principles and seeking one to lead us in their attainment, we extend to _____ a call to be our minister. We charge him/her to guide us in our worship, instruct us in our learning, sustain us in our suffering, share with us in our joys, challenge us in our deliberations, and abide with us in our frailties.

We pledge to him/her support for his/her ministry among us. We will provide for his/her economic needs and seek to sustain his/her spirits that he/she be not weary in his/her duties.

We therefore promise this day the best that is in us to him/her and to one another.

We would strive to fill our lives with zeal tempered by understanding, a sense of justice tempered by compassion, vision that seeks to enlighten the darkened corners of today's world, a yearning for peace which is militant in its longing, and, above all, an abiding sense of the presence of God, that we never turn from our highest calling.   (DRK)

C. Prayer for a Church Anniversary

(Alludes to Genesis 1:12 and Hebrews 11:1; 12:1; RSV)

O God, by whose Word the universe is being created,
    by whose brooding presence humankind comes to populate the earth,
    by whose tender compassion all persons are called,
    called, and recalled through your Word to relationship with you:
We thank you for all those who before us have lived in the faith and now, triumphant, live with you.
Only faith can guarantee the blessings that we hope for, or prove the existence of realities that at present remain unseen. It was for faith that our ancestors were commended.
Thank you for the faith of the founders of this congregation: *(list names).*
With so many witnesses in a great cloud on every side of us, we call on your abiding attention, love, and guidance that we may be your faithful people through another day, another week, another year.   (KFK)

Sacraments and Rites of the Church

A. Baptism Order

Introduction

We read in the gospels that, baptized by John, Jesus witnessed that all people should turn and accept the God who had already accepted them. We the friends and members of _____, now the Body of Christ, do here proclaim the same witness.

(Name), the God who has claimed every person as a beloved child will today speak for you as a beloved daughter/son.
The candidate and family come forward or is presented.

Thanksgiving Prayer

LEADER: God be with you
PEOPLE: And also with you.
LEADER: Let us give thanks to God.
PEOPLE: It is good to give God thanks and praise.
LEADER: We thank you, God, for the gift of water that brings us life and health. In the ancient waters your faithful servant Noah turned from death to life when he turned toward you. Your child Israel found you close at hand when it passed from death to life amidst the raging waters. In the river Jordan, Jesus received John's baptism and witnessed that we too should turn toward you.

Recalling now your same boundless love, we ask that you bless us and *(name)* as we baptize her/him with this water, that we might be your servants to the world, strong in trust and courageous in loyalty to you. Amen.

Questions

To the Candidate
(If adult) _____, God has claimed you and claims you now as a beloved daughter/son.

Do you and will you turn from the domain of death in which your choices entangle, confuse, and break you?

And do you turn to God whose eternal love we embody today as it was embodied by Jesus our Christ?

(If child) (name) _____ and _____ (parent[s]/family), God chooses *(name)* as a beloved daughter/son.

Do you promise to raise *(name)* as God's beloved daughter/son that she/he might turn from the domain of death in which her/his choices will entangle, confuse, and break her/him?

And do you promise to raise *(name)* that she/he might turn to God whose eternal love we embody today as it was embodied by Jesus our Christ?

To the Community
Do you, friends and members of _____, turn again from the domain of death and to the God of eternal love?

And will you be as the body of Christ embodying that love to *(name)* as she/he lives with us in service to all God's children?

Baptism

(Name), I baptize you in the name of Jesus, our Christ.

Prayer

God, Jesus embodied your eternal love in word and deed. Thank you for that gift.

We thank you also that today, as the Body of Christ, we can witness that same love to *(name)*, proclaiming that she/he is your beloved daughter/son. May you encourage us all in our life together, that we might find new ways to uncover your gracious presence in the world. Amen.

Reception (*Unison*)

We, the friends and members of _____, do hereby accept you into our church, which is called the Body of Christ. We do not presume to tell you what you must believe, for ours is a community of free inquiry and searching. We promise to share with you our experience of faith and ask that you share yourself with us. In this way we shall learn from one another, grow stronger, and more often be faithful to God as servants to all people. So be it!

Presentation

Sisters and brothers, may I present our new sister/brother in Christ, *(name)*.
(Suggested psalms: 18:1–7, 17; 27:1–9; 30:1–4, 11–13; 42; 124) (JWR)

Notes on the Baptismal Order

This order is based on Ph.D. research on the history of Christian worship.

It attempts to retain the classic shape for baptism that emerged in the second and third centuries and that has evolved since then. The Thanksgiving Prayer is an adaptation of Luther's famous baptismal "Flood Prayer," with its emphasis on life most intimately being our self-realization either for or against God. The baptismal questions echo the baptismal practices in the fourth century, in which faith was not so much belief as turning from Satan's domain to God's domain. Despite ecumenical concerns, the trinitarian baptismal formula, which cannot be made adequately inclusive and which imposes a certain theological view on a congregation, has been dropped in favor of the more apostolic formula, "in the name of Jesus." (JWR)

B. Communion Orders

Introduction

When Jesus sat at table and enjoyed communion with tax collectors and sinners he proclaimed that God's care knows no bounds. We proclaim again the comfort and challenge of that witness: all are invited now to share God's table, and be nourished by the Bread of Life.

Thanksgiving Prayer

LEADER: God be with you,

PEOPLE: And also with you.

LEADER: Lift up your hearts:

PEOPLE: We lift them up to God.

LEADER: Let us thank God:

PEOPLE: It is good to thank God.

LEADER: We thank you, God, that you have provided for all the worlds that ever were or will be by giving yourself to them in love. If we go to the heights of the mountains, or if we make the grave our bed, you are with us. If we go to the depths of the sea, your right hand holds us fast.

We thank you for Jesus, your Word, who lived among us, uncovering your presence. We thank you that you stamped his death with victory and that Life, not Death, was the final word.

We ask now that you bless us, as we share this bread and cup, that we might be nourished by that same unbounded love and so be encouraged to be your servants to the world.

And now, as your daughters and sons whom you have reconciled to yourself, we pray: *(Prayer of our Savior)*

Communion

(At breaking the bread)   As this grain once was scattered in the fields and has come together in one bread, so we, with different needs and hopes, come together as one, for we share one bread. Take. The Bread of Life.

(At pouring the cup)   The cup which we share is the cup of the New Covenant written in our hearts and witnessed by Jesus. Take. Drink. The Cup of the New Covenant. God is with you.

Prayer After Communion

Thank you, God, for renewing us at your table by the presence of our Christ. Thank you for your eternal love, the Bread of Life, that sustains all creation. May you continue to love us in our faithful acts and by that love discourage us from our unfaithful acts, that we might rejoice as your servants to the world. Amen. *(Suggested psalms: 34:1–8; 40:1–9; 63:1–8; 126; 131; 139:1–11)*

(JWR)

Notes on the Communion Order

This order is based on Ph.D. research on the history of Christian worship.

In the past twenty-five years New Testament scholars have suggested a more adequate understanding of the Supper that moves beyond the controversy of whether Jesus actually instituted "the Supper" or whether the early church handed down "mere legend." Perhaps the most decisive part of Jesus' ministry has been his sharing table with even the worst of people ("tax collectors and sinners"). At table, people realized faith in God and experienced the eschaton. The early church continued Jesus' table ministry with its Supper scene.

This communion order attempts to do justice to current understandings of Jesus' ministry while holding to the classic shape of communion. The Thanksgiving (eucharistic) Prayer retains classic elements of other similar prayers: recounting God's mighty works in history; effectively remembering Jesus' ministry; asking for God's presence to be realized in the community; and offering ourselves as disciples in the ministry that Jesus began. The Bread saying comes from 1 Corinthians 10 and Didache 9. The Cup saying comes from Jeremiah 31 and 1 Corinthians 11.

If the order seems bare, let its richness come from a joyous celebration. Jesus' table sharing was a festive event (Matthew 11:16–19). Sing and play joyous music. Use celebrative readings. Smile and give God the chance to rejoice in your joy. (JWR)

Communion Order *(Based on materials used at Grailville Women in Ministry Week, 1979; alludes to 1 Corinthians 10:16 and Luke 14:17, RSV)*

The Invitation

LEADER: The table is now prepared for us. We are invited to share in the feast of God's presence, celebrating here and now all that is meant by being alive.

The Spirit of God moves in and through all time, in every age, in every corner of the earth, calling people to renew their hope and joy.

PEOPLE: At this table we celebrate Jesus, who touched our brokenness with his life; who gathers us together, inside and out. We give ourselves to that wholeness, moving from hurt to happiness and from darkness to light, filling our lives with love, laughter, and each other, and joining with all created things to say: "Holy are you, O God."

The Peace

LEADER: The peace of God be with you always.
PEOPLE: And also with you.
(The clergy and congregation may greet one another in God's name with the greeting and response, "Peace be with you.")

The Eucharistic Prayer

LEADER: Holy are you, O God, for your mercy is endless. You have filled all creation with light and life, and your glory stretches through the heavens.

It was you who led Abraham and Sarah to the land of promise, who saved your people from the desert of bitter tears, who called them to the land of the living. It was you who blessed Miriam and David when they danced and sang in holy places. And through Jesus the Christ, you taught us to celebrate. Those who were blind saw the sun of your goodness, the crippled leaped for joy, and those who were locked in the prison of their fears were given the freedom to love.

PEOPLE: Your spirit calls us now, in this place, to gather all people into our celebration, to help the lame and blind, to wipe away tears with an outstretched hand.

LEADER: The bread of our being loved, the wine of our joy, stand as reminders that miracles in faith and risk continue to happen. In thanksgiving and remembrance, we ask you to bless this bread and wine so that, in sharing them together, we shall be your church.

The Sharing of the Bread and Wine

Through the broken bread we participate in the body of Christ. . . . *(Here the people may say the names of those who are brought with us, in spirit, to the table. A piece of bread may be broken for each.)* Come, for all things are ready. . . . Eat this, for it is the body of Christ, bread broken in love for you.

Through the cup of blessing we participate in the new life Christ gives. . . . Drink this, for it is the wine of our joy, flowing as a gift of God's spirit into our lives.
(During the distribution the congregation may join in singing such hymns as "Let Us Break Bread Together" or "One Bread, One Body.")

The Thanksgiving

LEADER: Let us give thanks.

PEOPLE: We give thanks, O God, because in your own free gift of love you have reached out to us. You have refreshed us at your table, touched our deepest needs, and called us to a life shared in memory and hope. Send us forth with courage and joy in the name of Jesus Christ, that we, too, may become bread and peace for one another and the world. Amen.

(MAN)

C. Other Resources for Communion Services

Calls to Worship

1. LITURGIST #1: Why is it that we come together like this? What is it that we think sharing some bread and wine can do to change the spaces that separate us from one another, and from God's world? We eat and drink with other people on many occasions.

   LITURGIST #2: How is it that the common act of eating—with strangers, even with enemies—can be transforming, healing, activating? Are we even sure we believe that can happen? Do we really want it to happen? Sometimes it feels like everyone wants worship to make the differences fade away in the wholeness, in God; sometimes it feels like everyone wants the colors of the rainbow to run like wet dye and mix. I can't come to worship for that, can you?

   LITURGIST #3: Let's worship God, with the hope instead that after all the winds and storms of being together, the colors of our various lives might appear, distinct, yet unified, like a rainbow. Let us worship in the hope that just for a moment, God's Spirit might shine through us to bring light and color to an often dark and complex world. I hunger for moments of wholeness like that. What about you?

PEOPLE: So be it. Yes, we hunger, not only for the rainbow to appear—bright and illuminating, but also that we might come to the end of this rainbow fed and ready again to meet wind and storm with hope—hope of clear skies and rainbows ahead, once more. (ME)

Note: This communion service was part of a Southern California Conference meeting of the UCC. Behind the altar was a huge rainbow reflecting the struggle to deal with ethnic/cultural diversity. The communion breads were from various ethnic traditions. (ME)

2. In every place, in every moment, God is present with us.

In this place, at this moment, we are called to be totally aware of God's presence.

Come, let us strip away every pretense and every defense, that we may be made new in communion with our God.

Come, let us worship God. (PM)

3. Christ is the bread of life.

We have nourished ourselves many times on God's word, yet we are hungry again.

Come, listen to God's promise.

Come, feast at God's table.

Let it renew your courage and satisfy your longings. (PM)

4. LEADER: Can God spread a table in the wilderness?
   PEOPLE: Can God give bread to the people?
   LEADER: We gather in the faith that the table is already prepared.
   PEOPLE: We gather in the knowledge that the bread of life is set before us.
   LEADER: Let us worship God. (MSG)

Invitation to Communion

Friends, God prepares a feast for you and all people; a feast of good things, a feast of peace. Come and taste. Eat and be filled. Drink deep and never thirst again. Come to the feast God prepares. (MAM)

Prayers of Confession

1. *(Call to confession)* When afraid of the unknown, we may miss the movement of God's Spirit. When captive to false authorities, we may lose the freeing power of God's truth. When we demand prestige for ourselves, we may disregard the authentic claims of servanthood. All that thus separates us from our

Creator and from one another is sin. Let us recognize and own up to the evil and wrong that both fascinates and torments us.

(Prayer of confession) We confess, O God, that we honor the popular and powerful and wander from your will and way. We are lost in the wilderness of our own desires, scarcely recognizing our thirst for more fulfilling purposes. In our longing to be important, we betray you. We have been insensitive to the needs of those near us and unmindful of the distress of sisters and brothers in other lands. Forgive us, Friend of Sinners, and help us put the past behind us. Free us to be responsible and to move toward the goals to which Christ calls us. Amen.

(Assurance of forgiveness) God offers rivers in the deserts of our arid lives, that we might recognize and honor the One who creates and provides. We are nourished in body and spirit at the table Christ sets before us. The evil of our past lives is wiped away. God is doing a new thing within us and among us. Move ahead in faith, praising God for the new life that is yours.   (LB)

2. *(Read Luke 14:16–24)* Gracious God, our lives are full of excuses that keep us away from the feast of life. We are too busy with work, activities, and private relationships. We have heard the call. We know a table of good things is prepared for us, but we do not answer the call to come to the table. We know it is not our excuses but our lives that you seek. Help us now to lay aside our excuses that we can come with joy to your banqueting table. Amen.

(MAM)

A Eucharistic Prayer

LEADER 1: Holy One, you speak to us in silence,
yet all languages interpret you.
Because you call us to be in community,
we are able to become gift to one another.
We invoke now your Holy Spirit
upon us and upon these gifts,
that in sharing them,
we may discern your presence which becomes our life.

LEADER 2: We remember and give you thanks for those called out with a vision of possibility and promise: for Abraham and Sarah, for Isaac and Rebecca, for Jaocb with Leah and Rachel, for Moses and Miriam. We thank you for your people who followed Moses through the birthing waters of the Red Sea into the wilderness of tempering search, until they became a people ready to enter the promised land.

LEADER 3: We thank you for the openness of Mary who dared to accept the call to be the bearer and nurturer of your Anointed One, Jesus. We bless you, O God, for Jesus, who through his life, crucifixion, death, and resurrection fully lived the promise of redemptive wholeness available for all who would be obedient to your creating will. Therefore we rejoice to proclaim:

ALL: Christ has died. Christ has risen. Christ will come again.

(EEB/RESR)

Prayer of Gratitude After Communion

Because the broken bread has meant our healing, because the outpoured cup has meant our life, because our common sharing has meant the communion of our souls, and because we have here been graced by your presence, God, we give you thanks and pray that our lives may be renewed in the life and the love of Jesus Christ. Amen. (DB)

Benediction

LEADER: Return to your homes, your work, your play, refreshed, renewed, and empowered.

PEOPLE: We have met the Christ in word and sacrament, in listening and sharing.

LEADER: Gather at other tables with friends and loved ones, knowing that Christ is there as well as here.

PEOPLE: We welcome the love and acceptance we know here and at other places where we break bread.

LEADER: All our moments and meetings can be sacramental, if we live in awareness of whose we are.

PEOPLE: We pray that our eyes may be opened and our spirits attuned to live in Christ. Amen. (LB)

Rites of the Church

A. For the Time of Passing and the Celebration of a Life: A Poem

(Alludes to Psalm 23)

My Hand in Thy Hand

When death comes quietly, the mystic close
of an old mystic legend, fully told,
the gradual days that strew the withering rose
and drape the forest aisles with bannered gold—
or when death comes, sudden and unaware,
a cold mist lifting to the morning sun,
an epilogue too soon, the stage left bare
of actors and the final scene undone:

Then Thou art with me, and Thy rod and staff
comfort me, and we journey—I and Thou—
on where the shadows deepen. More than half
my waking senses dimmed, I go handfast,
and on the other side friends wait me now.
Footfirm I go with all the terrors passed.   (WWW)

B. An Order for Christian Marriage

OFFICIANT: Dear family and friends, we are gathered here, amid the beauty of
nature, and in the presence of God, to unite _____ and _____ in
marriage. Let us pray: Maker of all beauty, who makes the sun to
rise in splendor, and to march in quiet radiance across the sky; who
has filled the face of the earth with trees, perfumed the flowers,
provided harmony to thought, and moral consciousness to character,
we rejoice in your perfection, and in the marvelous design that
unites us as families. Teach us to live in the beauty of your holiness
as known in Jesus Christ. Amen.

What _____ and _____ mean to each other is obvious in their
lives, but not easily expressed in the language of a ceremony. Marriage, and the union it symbolizes, can be the most intriguing of
human experiences, for in any accounting, love in its infinite mani-
festations is what life is all about. To share their lives, to encourage
creativity, inspire each other to reach beyond the limits of the ordinary . . . not at the expense of each partner's individuality, but
rather, by the strength of the common bond, this is the hope in
which _____ and _____ come to be married.

Through the wedding ritual, two persons declare publicly their
intent to enter into a relationship of enduring love. For the Christian, this occasion is not a spectacle, but worship; it is not a mere
formal observance, but a participation in the will of God for life. A
wedding is the celebration of the highest we know in love, the
pledging of the deepest fidelity, the expression of the highest aspiration. A relationship so sacred must not be entered into casually, but
thoughtfully and deliberately.

On this occasion, _____ and _____ come before family and
friends to affirm the choice they have made of each other as a life's
mate, and their intention to establish a home in the fulfillment of life
together. Out of this tangled world, they have been drawn together,
two people bound firmly by the sure insights of love.

Are you, _____, ready to enter this holy relationship, and to
accept the responsibilities of a wife, to be _____'s loving, faithful,
and supportive wife whether in days of success or adversity?

BRIDE: I am.

OFFICIANT: And are you, _____, ready to enter this holy relationship and to accept the responsibilities of a husband, to be _____'s loving, faithful, and supportive husband whether in days of success or adversity?

GROOM: I am.

OFFICIANT: By these answers, which you have given after due consideration and serious thought, your purpose and willingness to take one another for better or for worse, from this day forward, is affirmed.

Now, if you know of nothing legal or moral to forbid your union and you wish to take its vows, indicate that by joining your right hands.

Scripture Reading: 1 Corinthians 13

OFFICIANT: From the earliest time, the golden circle has been a symbol of wedded love. . . . It is made of pure gold to symbolize pure love. Being one unbroken circle, it symbolizes unending love. As often as either of you see this golden circle, you will be reminded of this high moment and the unending love you promise.

BRIDE and GROOM (one by one):

With this ring, I thee wed,
and pledge to share my life with you, loving and caring for you through all life's varying experiences.

OFFICIANT: Since you have promised your love to each other, and before God and these witnesses have exchanged these solemn vows, and these symbols of abiding love, I now pronounce you husband and wife. From now on each of you will see your own experiences in a new light as your life together unfolds. May you have courage to love each other, and by implication, all others on this earth, not only as you are, but as you are yet to be, with a love that is always new.

Let us pray: Gracious God, home of our spirits, grant to this couple true love to unite them spiritually, patience to assimilate their differences, forgiveness to cover their failures, guidance to lead them in the proper ways, courage to face perplexity, and inner peace to comfort them even in disillusionment and distress, throughout their lives. In Jesus' name, Amen.

And now, I invite all of you to be of the first to welcome _____ and _____ as partners in Christian marriage! (RDD)

C. The Parents' Blessing (Wedding Service)

PASTOR: Let us all remember that the path of love is meant to be walked together with all the human family. All love is nurtured and guided by the love of others. Each of us counts on relatives, friends, and neighbors for the caring and concern that replenishes our own ability to love. _____ and _____ marry this day in the midst of the affection and friendship of you all and, most especially, in the presence of those whose love has been their life's companion, their parents. I ask them

now for their blessing on the marriage of their children. *(First one set of parents, then the other is called by name and asked this question.)*
_____ and _____, do you give your blessing and promise the support of your love to the marriage of _____ and _____?

PARENTS: We do.

(ABD)

D. Wedding Prayers

1. Spirit of Life, your creative power is seen in the whole universe; in myriad stars and planets, and infinite space. And yet we dare to believe that you care for us and that you are mindful of the things that we do. In your presence we gather today, confirming a new constellation in human relationships—the marriage of _____ and _____. Let your Spirit be known among us, that we may do what we do here with our whole hearts and wills, and that the commitment _____ and _____ make to each other may be a sign of your love on earth. Amen.

(RCD)

2. Source and spring of all our joy and hope,
   By whose spirit our spirits are continually fed,
   Through whose mystery the meaning of our life is revealed,
   By whose knowledge we come to know ourselves:

   Be the abiding and unending presence with this man and this woman,
   When they know themselves to be deeply in love
   And when they feel estranged,
   When they experience elation,
   When they know despair.

   Because of your love that endures forever,
   May their care toward the larger world
        be shaped by all that is tender.
   May they discover that when they are faithful toward you and toward each other
   Even words that are critical fall with beauty upon the ear.

   Through the intensity of their life together
   May they discover words that nurture
                        gestures that heal
                        thoughts that illumine,
   Sharing those experiences
   That turn life itself
   Into one continuing act of praise,
   Through Jesus Christ. Amen.

(EEB)

Peacemaking

A. Calls to Worship

1. (*Paraphrases Psalm 101:1–2*, KJV)
   LEADER: I will sing of mercy and justice,
   PEOPLE: For mercy and justice are praises befitting God.
   LEADER: I will follow the way of mercy and justice, for it is the way to peace.
   PEOPLE: And on the seventh day peace was created; this is our sabbath, the day of peace, the aim of creation.
   ALL: Thanks be to God!

   (KAS)

2. (*Paraphrases Isaiah 2:4; 52:7*, RSV)
   LEADER: How beautiful upon the mountains are the feet of those who bring good news,
   PEOPLE: Who publish peace, who bring good tidings, who publish salvation, and proclaim, "Your God reigns!"
   LEADER: God will judge between many peoples,
   PEOPLE: And they shall beat their swords into plowshares and nation shall not lift up sword against nation: neither shall they learn war any more.
   ALL: Let us lift up our voices and praise the God of peace and justice. Amen.

   (RCD)

3. (*Based on Psalm 33*, RSV)
   LEADER: Let us rejoice together in the God of justice and righteousness.
   PEOPLE: Let us sing a new song to God, making melody with strings and voices.
   LEADER: How happy is the nation who trusts in God!
   PEOPLE: How happy are those who hope in God's holy name!
   LEADER: A ruler is not saved by a great army; a warrior is not delivered by great strength.
   PEOPLE: Stockpiles of weapons are powerless to win peace.
   LEADER: But God is faithful to the reverent, whose hope is in God's steadfast love.
   PEOPLE: We wait for God, our help and shield.
   ALL: Let your steadfast love, O God, be upon us, even as we hope in you. Amen.

   (RCD)

B. Prayers of Confession

1. All other creatures praise you and reflect your glory by being what they were created to be. Yet we, who are made in your image, are like shattered and warped mirrors. We have turned your creativity into a tool for making instruments of destruction and mechanisms which damage the earth. We have debased

your delight in the goodness of all creation into personal pleasure gained at the expense of other creatures. We have warped your order for the interrelationships of all being into a scheme for making all being center on ourselves. We have split the unity of humankind into many self-conscious groups which come together to play roles in dramas which we have written for ourselves. We confess that we have not permitted your image as present in the Incarnate One to invade, engage, and enliven our imaginations.

Have mercy upon us. Do not leave us alone. Challenge us anew with the vision of what we might become. Amen. (DRB)

2. (*Paraphrases Luke 14:11; 22:27;* RSV) Enemies? Who has enemies? Yet there are certain people we love so little: people who want no good to come to us; folks whom we deliberately ignore and insult. Yes, we have personal enemies. On the national and international level it is no better. God, forgive us. Burn into our cold hearts the heat of the truth that to love neighbor is to love you, that we cannot love you without loving our neighbors. Convince us that those who humble themselves shall be exalted and those who exalt themselves over others shall be made low. For we want to be faithful disciples of Jesus, who came among us as one who serves. Amen. (KFK)

3. O God, whose heart weeps at the disobedience and the suffering of any of your creatures, look with justice and mercy on the prominent trouble spots of your globe. You be the champion of those suffer poverty, dislocation, hunger, and disease. You be the chastisement of those who abuse innocent victims. Unerring judge of us all, forgive us our involvement in the sins of your people, whether it be by action direct or indirect. Renew in us the will to make peace and do justice that we may bring you delight, not tears. Amen. (KFK)

4. Call to Confession

Jesus calls us to come, holding nothing in our hands, confessing our need of God.

Prayer

God of true peace, we confess that we have preferred the peace the world gives over that which you offer. We have often sought the peace of worldly security and social conformity over the challenge and fulfillment of discipleship to Jesus Christ. Forgive us and deepen our trust in you, that we may give ourselves to the adventure of living in faith. Make us responsive and responsible to your Holy Spirit, through the grace of Jesus Christ. Amen.

Proclamation of God's Grace

This is the Good News! In Jesus Christ God forgives us and returns the lives we have offered, overflowing with new life. Amen. (RCD)

5. Gracious Holy One of every place and time, we ask you to listen to us, your children, and to free us from our own unwillingness to listen. We want to live in your hope, having the courage to care for the world around us. But so many things frighten us, God. In the fear of our own poverty, we clutch on to all we

have, rather than sharing who we are. In our fear of war, we shut our door on our neighbors, instead of being your makers of peace. In our fear of who we are, we try to pretend that we don't need other people, even when we are longing for your love. Heal our fear, God, help us to know of your presence with us. Amen. (SEG)

6. Gracious God, you have promised to be our security. Yet we deny your presence with us, and we keep chasing after false gods all around us. We create images made of metal and pretend that they give us protection. We ignore those who need us, and surround ourselves instead with walls of false security. We need your love to change our lives in hope. Bring your grace upon us, God. Amen. (SEG)

7. O God, our reconciler, we come before you as a people of folly, who have sought the wisdom of the world. We have built arms and prepared for war, thinking that will bring us peace and security. Yet we find ourselves an anxious people, isolated from one another and from you. We have sought to make ourselves great by pointing out the evil in others. Yet we confess that we, too, are stained with evil. Help us, O God, to know not the folly of the world but the wisdom of Christ, who is our hope. Amen. (KAS)

8. O God, we have looked and looked for you. Yet we cannot see you. We have strained our eyes to see your salvation and to look for your outstretched hand. Yet we are still floundering in deep waters. We have forgotten, O God, that you have come in the ones least expected. You have come as a foreigner. You have come as a beggar. You have come as one who hungers and thirsts. You have come as a lowly Jewish man in the midst of the mighty Roman Empire. You have presented yourself in the least. No wonder we have not seen you trying to save us. We have looked only for the mighty and the spectacular instead of for the lowly and the poor. Forgive us, O God, for looking past you. Amen.

(KAS)

9. Lover of the Universe, we come to you now believing that your all-embracing care is for each one of us, individually and particularly, as well as for all the multitudes through time and space. We confess that we have often blocked out of our lives either the awareness or the practice of your love.

We have tried to live as if we were the center of all creation. We have pretended that our darkness is a light for others to follow. We have sought wisdom in high places, not among ordinary people or events. We have missed seeing Christ in other people. We have failed to represent Jesus in our encounters with one another.

We seek to hear again the assurance of your forgiveness. We ask for the capacity to accept your forgiveness and embrace the freedom given us to begin anew as disciples of Christ and as apostles of good news. Amen. (LB)

10. The Corporate Confession

We confess that we have turned away from you, O God, and forgotten that you are our peace and hope. We have put our trust in our businesses, our organizations, our politics, and our incomes to order our lives and our society. We continue to trust in the structures of oppression that ensure us privilege rather than in your promise of redeeming love and peace.

We confess that we are members of a church called Christian that speaks with a whisper amid the clamor of militarism and injustice. Forgive us for the sin of sloth.

We confess that we have taken the major share of the world's resources from the daily needs of people and have used them to make credible our threat to commit mass murder. We allow others to live in abject squalor so that we can be power brokers of a nuclear nightmare. We fear to repent, knowing that the result will be the freedom to live with boldness and integrity in a world where the only hope—the only security—is you.

Forgive us for the sin of pride.

Silent Prayer

Words of Assurance

God is even now giving us the gift of repentance. God is at work in the world. It is not we who hope, but God who hopes in us.   (WUMC)

C. Unison Prayers

1. *(The last petition is from the hymn "God of Grace and God of Glory" by H.E. Fosdick)*
As a nation we are prone to fight, though we say we seek not conflict but freedom for ourselves and for others. We take on the burden of costly defense, when the risk of peace without violence is a response closer to your will. The bugle call to arms is easier to hear than the wistful solo voice of peace, goodwill to all people.

We know our minds! But do we?

You, who love us in our fragmentation and in our wholeness, who love us in our purposefulness and in our wandering, let us see our places in the one human family. Give to us and our leaders the energies to pursue freedom, justice, equality. Save us from our warring madness. Amen.   (KFK)

2. God, your compassion is for all people and all creation. Help us to share the burden of your heart concerning our troubled and violent world. Teach us to trust in you more than in the technology of destruction, that we may be peacemakers, like Jesus the Christ. Amen.   (RCD)

3. *(Alludes to Luke 18:1–8, RSV)*   Righteous God, the human cry comes before you day and night. We long for peace and justice, for love and truth on the earth. Teach us to pray, never losing courage; teach us humility, that our prayers may be worthy. May Christ come into our lives, and your reign of righteousness be established among us, through the power of the Holy Spirit. Amen.

(RCD)

4. *(Alludes to 1 Corinthians 1:18–25, RSV)*   Wise and powerful God, give us the courage to acknowledge our weakness; grant us the wisdom to recognize our

foolishness and to turn to you. Through Jesus Christ, bring your wisdom and your power into our lives, that we may join you in responsibility for healing the sufferings of the world. May we share in the quest to bring your future into our present, to bring your day of justice and love into this unjust and unloving world. Amen. (BP)

5. God of peace and justice, enable us to hear your Word not only in scripture, but also in the voices of your people as they cry out for food, for freedom from oppression, for a lasting justice and peace. Free us from fear and hatred, from suspicion and prejudice, that we may come to see all persons as your children. We thank you for the blessings of our lives. We ask that you show us ways to begin sharing these generous gifts with others who may be less fortunate, but no less deserving of your *shalom*. We ask these things in the name of Jesus, who lived humbly and died an outcast, that we might know your concern for the poor and outcast among us. Amen. (BP)

6. (*Alludes to Matthew 5:9*, RSV)   We come before you, God of all nations and peoples, knowing how human warfare, strife, and contention grieves you. We offer ourselves as instruments of your peace. Fill us with the vision of a world at one, and guide our actions, that we may be counted among the peacemakers, your true children, who follow Jesus the Christ. Amen.
(RCD)

D. Litanies

1. Social Justice   (*Paraphrases Galatians 3:27–28*, RSV)

LEADER: You are all children of God
PEOPLE: through faith in Christ Jesus,
LEADER: For as many of you as were baptized into Christ
PEOPLE: have put on Christ.
LEADER: There is neither Jew
PEOPLE: nor Greek.
LEADER: There is neither slave
PEOPLE: nor free person;
LEADER: There is no male and female,
UNISON: For you are all one in Christ Jesus.

Silent Prayer

Collect

God, your love which proclaims all people equal was proclaimed to us at our baptism. May we incarnate that love by making equal and just whatever is not. Amen.

Confession of Equality (*Unison*)

God, we know that every person is your beloved child. When anyone suffers, you suffer also. May we have the courage to bring equality among people so that

your life, as well as ours, is free from the pain of injustice. Amen.
Scripture Readings: Micah 6:6–8; Luke 6:43–45; Galatians 3:26–28   (JWR)

2. Litany for Disarmament   *(Paraphrases Matthew 6:10; Leviticus 26:6; and Amos 5:24; RSV; alludes to Isaiah 2:1–4; 9:6; 11:9; 35:9; RSV; unison portion translated and adapted from a prayer by Rabbi Nachman of Bratzlav, 1770–1811)*

LEADER: O God of peaceful purpose, who has given us the Prince of Peace, Jesus Christ, to show us the ways that lead to life, not death, to you we lift our prayer.

PEOPLE: God of peace, may your reign come; your will be done on earth, as in heaven.

LEADER: From the wonderful stuff of created order, we conceive and build weapons designed to destroy what you have created.

PEOPLE: God of peace, may your reign come; your will be done on earth, as in heaven.

LEADER: Peoples and nations fear the mushroom-shaped cloud, their resources are plundered in the race for armed supremacy, and plans for destruction proliferate, while plans for peace fall by the way.

PEOPLE: God of peace, may your reign come; your will be done on earth, as in heaven.

LEADER: In our time, children become the victims of war: Left homeless or oppressed, emotionally maimed, disfigured by shrapnel and shell, orphaned and killed.

PEOPLE: God of peace, may your reign come; your will be done on earth, as in heaven.

LEADER: We your people around the world gather in houses of worship great and small, urban, suburban and rural, in the midst of these forces and specters, asking . . . pleading . . . that your Spirit will be present with those who represent the nations when they sit down to negotiate limitations in weapons poised at the heartland—the heart—of the other, that they may discover the miracle of dialogue, and achieve victories for peace beyond their expectations.

PEOPLE: God of peace, may your reign come; your will be done on earth, as in heaven.

UNISON: May we see the day when war and bloodshed cease, when a great peace will embrace the world, when nation will not threaten nation, and humankind will not again make war, when all who inhabit this world shall realize that we have not come into being in order to hate, or to destroy. We have come into being to praise, to labor, to love. Compassionate God, bless the leaders of all nations with the power of compassion. Fulfill the promise conveyed in scripture: I will bring peace to the land, and you shall lie down and no one shall terrify you. I will rid the land of vicious beasts and it shall not be ravaged by war. Let love and justice flow like a mighty stream. Let peace fill the earth as the waters fill the sea. Amen.   (DBB)

3. Litany for Peace

LEADER: Creator and Ruler of life, who has given us the Prince of Peace, let us begin our press for peace in the world by accepting the inner peace you offer to our lives.

PEOPLE: Give us your peace, O God.

LEADER: Let us be makers of peace within our own families and communities.

PEOPLE: Give us your peace, O God.

LEADER: Fill our hearts with a love of humankind and respect for human dignity that will demand justice and peace for all the world.

PEOPLE: Let us have peace, O God.

LEADER: Guide your church, O God, to a concern for world peace, and let us accept our responsibility to call our nation and others to commit themselves to a strategy for peace.

PEOPLE: Help us make peace, O God.

LEADER: Lead us in our press for peace, that we may not cease until there is truly peace on earth.

PEOPLE: Help us make peace, O God. Amen. (PM)

4. World Order Sunday *(Alludes to Genesis 1:1–2 and Isaiah 11:6–7, RSV)*

LEADER: "In the beginning God created the heavens and the earth. The earth was without form and void, and darkness was upon the face of the deep; and the Spirit of God was moving over the face of the waters."

PEOPLE: Out of chaos came a natural order of animals and plants and even the universe being in harmony with itself until . . .

LEADER: We developed spears, guns, and missiles that would create not a symphony of peace, but the discord of pain, of blood, of loss.

PEOPLE: It is not God who has abandoned us but rather it is we who have turned our backs on a loving God and have wandered into the wilderness of despair, apathy, and even death.

LEADER: May order be restored to our broken world; show us, God, how each of us can contribute to a more peaceful world,

PEOPLE: A world in which the lion may lie down with the lamb, in which people see one another as sisters and brothers, a world of communal sharing and caring. Praise and glory be to the living and loving Christ, who offers us this new creation. Amen. (JH)

E. My Prayer After Hearing the Evening News

God, Creator of this spinning globe,
    peopled by humankind,
    all of whom you love,
hear us on this new day,
    at the beginning of an era
    that is potentially fearsome and dangerous.

Forgive us as individuals;
    forgive us as congregations,
    as congresses,
    state departments,
    presidents,
    prime ministers,
    parliaments,
    as common, ordinary, citizens.

Forgive our reliance upon ourselves and
    our own resources
    for the management of our disagreements.

Forgive us our dependence on violence
  for settling our conflicts.
God, you enter Afghanistan,
    Iran, Russia, and America
    to change their minds and hearts
    —to change ours.

Change us.
Change us from defenseless
    to defended,
    from fearful
    to confident,
from closed
    to open,
from shaken
    to courageous,
in the risk and work of establishing
    peace, justice, and equality
right here,
over there,
everywhere.   (KFK)

F. Affirmation of Faith

(*Quotes Isaiah 2:4; Matthew 5:9; and 2 Corinthians 5:19;* RSV)
LEADER: Isaiah said:
    "It shall come to pass that the peoples
    shall beat their swords into plowshares,
    and their spears into pruning hooks;
    nation shall not lift up sword against nation,
    neither shall they learn war anymore."
PEOPLE: This is our vision:
    That a world of harmony and peace

will replace our world
of injustice and war.

LEADER: Jesus said:
"Blessed are the peacemakers,
for they shall be called children of God."

PEOPLE: This is our calling:
To know God's ways of peace,
and so to make peace,
in our family and community,
our nation and world.

LEADER: Paul said:
"In Christ God was reconciling the world . . .
not counting their trespasses against them,
and entrusting to us the message of reconciliation."

PEOPLE: This is our faith:
That in Jesus,
we meet the God who makes peace
with our wayward and hurting world;
and that by this reconciling love,
we are moved to bridge the chasms
of fear and estrangement.

ALL: May it be so. Amen. (MLP)

G. Benediction

God give you peace, neither impotence nor cowardice, to replace loneliness with friendship, hatred with respect, war with justice, dishonesty with integrity, lust with love, hell with heaven. Amen. (KFK)

Key to Contributors

AAW	Ann Asper Wilson	LGS	Lyta G. Seddig
ABD	Ann B. Day	LME	Linda Mines Elliot
ARE	Arnold R. Enslin	LS	Laurie Simon
BHG	Brewster H. Gere	MAM	Mary Anne Morefield
BJW	Bonnie Jones-Witthun	MAN	Mary Ann Neevel
BP	Barbara Peterson	ME	Mitzi Eilts
BS	Betty Sarff	MLP	Michael L. Pennanen
CHS	Charlotte H. Still	MLS	Mary Lois Stansbery
DB	David Beebe	MSG	Mary Sue Gast
DBB	David B. Bowman	NRM	Nancy R. McMaster
DBR/ JCN	David B. Royer and Jonathan C. Nelson	PM	Peggy McClanahan
		RAF	Rebecca A. Ferguson
DLM	Donald L. Metz	RCD	Ruth C. Duck
DRB	Daniel R. Bechtel	RDD	Roxanne D. Dunkel- berger
DRK	Dennis R. Knight		
EEB	Edwin E. Beers	RDS	Roger D. Straw
GER	Glen E. Rainsley	RESR	Ruth E.S. Robinson
HAS	Hilda A. Spann	RHM	Robert H. Midgley
HWW	Holly W. Whitcomb	RLA	Robert L. Anderson
JAP	Jeanne Audrey Powers	RNE	Richard N. Eick
JB	James Burd	RWD	Robert W. Duke
JCW	Jann C. Weaver	SEG	Sandra E. Graham
JH	James Hill	SLB	Sally L. Bartling
JHY	Junior High Youth, United Church of Christ, Union City, Michigan	SRH	Susan Ricketts Huff- man
		VSS	V. Shirley Stoos
		WRW	William R. Wolfe
JWR	John W. Riggs	WUMC	Wheadon United Methodist Church, Evanston, Illinois
KAS	Keith A. Schuette		
KCHS	Karen C.H. Sorensen		
KFK	Karl F. Kirkman Jr.	WWW	Wallace W. Winchell
LB	Lavon Bayler		